MASTERPIECES OF JEWISH AMERICAN LITERATURE

MASTERPIECES OF JEWISH AMERICAN LITERATURE

Sanford Sternlicht

Greenwood Introduces Literary Masterpieces

GREENWOOD PRESS
Westport, Connecticut • London

Library of Congress Cataloging-in-Publication Data

Sternlicht, Sanford V.
   Masterpieces of Jewish American literature / Sanford Sternlicht.
      p. cm. — (Greenwood introduces literary masterpieces, ISSN 1545–6285)
   Includes bibliographical references and index.
   ISBN-13: 978–0–313–33857–1 (alk. paper)
   ISBN-10: 0–313–33857–4 (alk. paper)
      1. American literature—Jewish authors. 2. Jews—United States—
Literary collections. 3. Judaism and literature—United States. 4. American
literature—Jewish authors—History and criticism.   I. Title.
PS508.J4M37   2007
810.8'08924—dc22   2006038252

British Library Cataloguing in Publication Data is available.

Library of Congress Catalog Card Number: 2006038252
ISBN-13: 978–0–313–33857–1
ISBN-10: 0–313–33857–4
ISSN: 1545–6285

First published in 2007

Greenwood Press, 88 Post Road West, Westport, CT 06881
An imprint of Greenwood Publishing Group, Inc.
www.greenwood.com

Printed in the United States of America

The paper used in this book complies with the
Permanent Paper Standard issued by the National
Information Standards Organization (Z39.48–1984).

10 9 8 7 6 5 4 3 2 1

For Mary Beth, Linette, and Rachel

Contents

9   Philip Roth, *Portnoy's Complaint* (1969)   111

10   Cynthia Ozick, *The Messiah of Stockholm* (1987)   119

     Selected Bibliography   127

     Index   129

Preface

Masterpieces of Jewish American Literature is a study of 10 extremely important landmark novels by 10 major Jewish American writers. It provides insights into the writers' lives, backgrounds, and milieu. The works have been selected on the basis of artistic merit, historical significance, Jewish content, and accessibility for students and the general reading public. The studies are presented in order of publication date of the novels. The chronology spans most of the twentieth century.

Each chapter covers biographical context, plot development, character development, themes, narrative style, and historical context. Each chapter concludes with a bibliography for the writer and the novel. A selected general bibliography at the end of the text provides additional reading opportunities on the subject of modern Jewish American literature.

Masterpieces of Jewish American Literature provides the reader with an understanding of the achievement and scope of modern Jewish American writing that deeply informed and enhanced American literature from the beginning of the twentieth century to the present.

Acknowledgments

My deep gratitude to the staff of Syracuse University Library, the staff of The College of Arts and Sciences' Computing Services, and my colleagues in Syracuse University's English Department. Three research assistants—Brendan Abel, Robert A. Tumas, and Kristen Vescera—were of inestimable aid on this project. As always, I am in awe of the patience of my partner, Mary Beth Hinton. She seemed never to tire of reading the drafts of the manuscript of this book.

Backgrounds

JEWISH LITERARY TRADITIONS

The Jews have long been known as the People of the Book. After the fall of Jerusalem and the destruction of the Temple by the Romans in 70 c.e., the inhabitants of Judea continued to revolt until the final conquest in 135 c.e. when the remnants of the nation were scattered to the four corners of the known world and the Jewish diaspora of 2,000 years began. It was their great book, the Hebrew Bible, known to others as the Old Testament, that, more than anything else, kept the religion and the culture alive. And the Bible has narratives, the first Jewish stories. The post-Jerusalem Jews also had the narratives, the wisdom, and the legends of the Talmud, the great commentary on the Bible and religious practice, begun in the fifth century c.e.

A great theme in Jewish literature is that of exodus. Jewish history has many of them: the exodus from Egypt led by Moses that brought the Israelites to the Promised Land of Canaan; expulsions from medieval England, France, and Germany in the time of the Crusades; the expulsion of the Spanish Jews in 1492 from the land they had lived in for hundreds of years; the exodus, after a sojourn of 500 years, stoked by pograms and race hatred, of two million Jews from Russia and the nations of Eastern Europe in the mass emigration to America from 1881 to 1924; and the flight of tens of thousands of survivors of the Holocaust to Palestine—some on a vessel named *Exodus*—after liberation from the German concentration camps in 1945.

Thus, the sense of impermanence has never left the life or the literature of Jews. They have always faced the sorrows, the suffering, the traumas, and the loss of relocation. Only in America did the end of the journey result in acceptance and security. One might think that the Jewish American immigrant narrative would always have a happy ending, but that is not so. The theme of loss of Jewish identity, often through assimilation in the younger generations, is a painfully recurring one. Lastly, the theme of changing, confusing choices pervades Jewish American imaginative writing to this day: differing generational values, a religious life in Brooklyn or Israel, old socialist ideals, or American capitalist enterprising.

The first Jewish literature in America was in Yiddish, the mother tongue of Eastern European Jewry. The writers first adored by immigrants, Mendele Mocher Sforim (1836–1917), I. L. Peretz (1851–1915), and Sholom Aleichem (1859–1916), were storytellers from Europe, as was the popular novelist Sholem Asch (1880–1957). Surely the greatest Yiddish writer to come from Poland to the United States was the Nobel Laureate Isaac Bashevis Singer (1904–1991). The old narratives and the new stories in Yiddish from the pen of Jewish Americans were widely disseminated through Yiddish language newspapers such as the *Jewish Daily Forward*. Besides Singer and his older brother Israel Joshua Singer (1893–1944) other important Jewish American writers in Yiddish include Morris Winchevsky (1856–1932), Morris Rosenfeld (1862–1923), David Edelstadt (1866–1892), and Joseph Boshover (1873–1915). And there were many new Americans writing in Hebrew too.

JEWISH LIFE IN AMERICA

Because the year of his departure for the New World, 1492, was the same year the Jews were expelled from Spain, some Jews may have been in hiding among Columbus's crew and entourage. But documented Jewish life in America began in 1654 when 23 Sephardic Jews (descendents of expelled Spanish Jews) arrived in Dutch New Amsterdam as refugees from Brazil, where the Portuguese had installed the Inquisition. Allowed to stay, they started a congregation and encouraged other Jews to join them. When the English captured the city in 1664 and renamed it New York, the Jews were again permitted to remain. In 1740 Parliament passed a law allowing citizenship for Jews living in British colonies.

During the American Revolution, Jews fought on the side of the rebels and helped to finance the Continental Congress. In the census of 1790 there were 1,500 Jews in the United States. The number in 1820 was 3,000. In 1826 Jews in New York were permitted to hold political office. Other states followed suit. Ten years later there were 6,000 Jews in the country, mostly of Sephardic origin. Now large numbers of Jews began to arrive from the German states due to unrest there, and by 1860 the Jewish population of the United States was 150,000. Many of these German Jews began as peddlers or small businessmen in New York City and then went into manufacturing—especially clothing. Some established large department stores in major cities such as New York, Philadelphia, and Boston. When the Civil War broke out in 1861, many Jews joined the Union army and a few joined the Confederate army. Judah Benjamin, a former U.S. Senator, became the Attorney General of the Confederacy and later Secretary of State. In 1880 250,000 Jews were living in the United States.

When Czar Alexander II of Russia was assassinated in 1881, massive pogroms caused a vast emigration of Jews to the United States. Eventually, two million Jews left Russia and Eastern European countries and crossed the Atlantic in the steerage of large passenger vessels. Most initially settled on the Lower East Side of Manhattan, a traditional immigrant area; large numbers of German and Irish immigrants had settled there earlier in the nineteenth century and their descendants had moved on. The exodus of Eastern European Jews was a momentous event in Jewish American history. Most Jewish Americans today are descendents of those intrepid voyagers.

Jews who came to America in the 1882–1924 period joined the expanding American labor force. Most became urban workers. In fact, almost all worked for wages: grandparents, parents, single women, single men, and children. Mothers with small children kept house in crowded, unsanitary apartments. They prepared meals, did wash by hand, tended the frequently ill children and adults, and took in piecework, or shared pushcart labor with their husbands to add to the family income.

Male immigrants who had no urban work skills and who spoke no English joined the workforce at the lowest levels. Some single men became pack peddlers, who purchased, at wholesale prices, dry goods, trinkets, and patent medicines for all ailments and then walked the back yards of city tenements, calling out their wares to housewives who would invite them to their flat if they desired a purchase. The peddlers needed very little capital to start their minuscule businesses. Some enterprising peddlers took enormous packs on trains to Upstate New York, New England, and even the South, selling their goods to farmers' wives and in villages where they were welcome. A few of these men found towns of their liking, and brought their families there as they established small businesses such as general dry goods, clothing, or furniture stores, and junkyards. Their grandchildren would become respected business people and civic leaders in their communities, and their children, professionally educated, left the small towns and moved to great cities: New York, Chicago, Los Angeles, and others.

Those men, and many women, who were not single, and who could or would not leave their families behind—having no marketable skills like tailoring—turned to the famous entry-level business opportunity: the pushcart. Young women found work in service to the more affluent German-Jewish families, or they found employment sewing in the garment industry sweatshops, where conditions and pay were terrible, but they made enough money in season to buy some fashionable clothing and save for a dowry. Men also worked in the garment industry as machine operators, owning their own sewing machines and carrying them to work each day. Children helped their mothers with piecework. If the family had a small business, everyone helped. The Jewish pioneers on the urban frontier had hard lives indeed.

The Jewish Publication Society was established in Philadelphia in 1888 for the publication of religious and secular books in Hebrew, Yiddish, and English. In 1892 the American Jewish Historical Society was founded in New York City.

On the Lower East Side Jewish clothing manufacturers, standardizing sizes, were turning out huge, mass-produced quantities of low-priced clothing for the American market, and for the first time most Americans could purchase ready-made clothes at affordable prices.

The year 1884 was a traumatic year for American Jews and for Jews the world over. It was the year of the beginning of the notorious Dreyfus Affair. Captain Alfred Dreyfus of the French army was falsely accused and convicted of being a spy for the Germans. The trial caused outbreaks of violence against Jews in France, a democratic nation. Jews in the United States and in Europe wondered if they were safe from racial hatred anywhere in the world. Dreyfus was sentenced to life imprisonment in the French penal colony on Devil's Island, off the Coast of French Guiana. Eventually, Dreyfus was exonerated and released, but the anti-Semitism exposed by the trial caused Theodor Herzl to call the First Zionist Congress in 1897, an action that led to the establishment of Jewish settlements in Palestine and eventually to the estab-lishment of the State of Israel.

In 1897 Abraham Cahan, a journalist, author, and social activist, founded the *Jewish Daily Forward*, the greatest of the many Yiddish newspapers of the twentieth century. The census of 1900 showed over one million Jews living in the United States. The following year saw the beginning of the *Jewish Encyclopedia*, and three years after that the Jewish Museum in New York City opened.

In 1913 a second foreign event, this one in Kiev, a city in Russian Ukraine, caused great anger and despair for American Jews and Jews the world over. A poor Jewish worker named Mendel Beiliss was arrested and falsely accused of murdering a Christian child with the intention of harvesting blood for ritual purposes. In the Middle Ages many Christians believed that Jews killed Christian children in order to use their blood in Jewish rituals. It was nonsense of course, but the finding of a murdered Christian child could provoke a general pogrom. Thus, another flood of anti-Semitism engulfed Russia. After a long imprisonment and trial, Beiliss was exonerated. In 1966 Bernard Malamud used the Beiliss blood libel case as the basis for his novel *The Fixer*.

Also in 1913 another infamous trial occurred in Atlanta, Georgia. Leo Frank, a Jewish businessman, was accused of the murder of a 14-year-old girl working for him, and despite his plea of innocence, he was found guilty of murder on the dubious testimony of one person, an employee. It seemed to Jews that if Frank were not Jewish, he would not have been so easily convicted. He was sentenced to death. The streets of Atlanta, a major American city, echoed with the cry "Kill the Jew!" The governor of Georgia was dubious about the verdict, and, to avoid a fatal miscarriage of justice, he commuted the sentence to life imprisonment. A lynch mob then broke into the prison and murdered Frank, whose innocence was posthumously established. Jewish Americans had protested and editorialized against the lynching of African Americans in the South and elsewhere. Now a Jew had been lynched. Questions arose in Jewish minds: Was America really a refuge from persecution after all?

The Dreyfus Affair in France, the Beiliss blood libel in Russia, the Frank lynching in the American South, the rise of violent anti-Semitism in Nazi Germany beginning in 1933, growing anti-Semitism in the United States in the 1930s, and, finally, the news of the Holocaust contributed to the growing belief of American Jews that they too needed the security of a homeland.

In 1916 Louis Brandeis became the first of a distinguished line of Jewish Supreme Court justices. American entry into World War I in 1917 brought tens of thousands of young Jewish men into the army and navy. Most served in France, many with distinction. That same year a great many American Jews viewed the Russian Revolution and the overthrow of the despotic Romanoff dynasty with favor, but the continuing injustices and brutalities of the communist regime eventually turned the majority against the new regime. The 1920 census found 3.5 million Jews living in the United States.

Immigrant Jewish businessmen from New York City did much to establish the American motion picture industry. In 1923 Marcus Loew and Louis

B. Mayer established the Metro-Goldwyn-Mayer Corporation (MGM). The Stock Market Crash in 1929 followed by the Great Depression impoverished hundred of thousands of American Jews, as the cities of the United States suffered unemployment rates of over 25 percent. In 1933, as Hitler and the Nazis came to power, Albert Einstein fled to the United States. World War II began in Europe in 1939, and American Jews began to hear reports of the beginning of the Holocaust. The next year the census indicated that the Jewish population of the United States had reached four million.

In 1941 the United States entered World War II, and hundreds of thousands of Jewish Americans served in the armed forces. When the war ended in 1945 and the extent of the Holocaust became apparent, American Jews sunk into a long period of grief for the loss of six million of their co-religionists and the disappearance of European Jewry in the lands of their forefathers. But 1948 brought elation as well as anxiety at the founding of the State of Israel by the United Nations, and its successful defensive against Arab aggression. Israeli victories in 1956, 1967, and 1973 assured them that the Jewish homeland would survive.

The 1951 conviction and 1953 execution of Soviet spy Julius Rosenberg and his wife, Ethel Rosenberg, brought fears of an outbreak of anti-Semitism in the United States of the McCarthy Period, but it did not happen. In 1960 the publication of Nobel Peace Prize winner Eli Wiesel's *Night* opened the floodgates of Holocaust memoirs, histories, and literature. The 1963 publication of Betty Friedan's *The Feminine Mystique* led to the founding, three years later, of the National Organization for Women (NOW) and the Women's Movement in America and throughout the world.

Neil Simon in 1965 began his reign as King of American Comedy with the stage version of *The Odd Couple*. That same year the Vatican repudiated Jewish collective guilt for the execution of Jesus. In 1974 Henry Kissinger, once a refugee from Nazi Germany, became the first Jew appointed U.S. Secretary of State. Saul Bellow won the Nobel Prize for Literature in 1976, and the next year Woody Allen, the cinema schlemiel, produced his most famous film: *Annie Hall*. Isaac Bashevis Singer received the Nobel Prize for Literature in 1978. The 1980 census showed a Jewish population of six million.

American Jews were upset over the conviction of Jonathan Pollard for spying for Israel in 1987. They feared that many Americans would wrongly believe that their first loyalty was to a foreign state. Pollard languishes in prison to this date. In 1989 Howard Nemerov became the United States' first Jewish Poet Laureate. That year the *Seinfeld* television epic began. The great memorial to the Jewish victims of Nazi Germany, the Holocaust Museum in Washington, D.C., opened in 1993, and the next year Steven Spielberg's film *Schindler's List* received the Best Picture Academy Award. Senator Joseph Lieberman, the Democratic Party candidate for vice president, was defeated in the election of 2000. The next year New York and all the American people grieved over the destruction of the twin towers of the World Trade Center and the loss of almost 3,000 lives. In the summer of 2006 Jews everywhere were stunned by the beginning of another Israeli–Arab conflict when Israeli soldiers were kidnapped and Arab terrorists from Lebanon directed missile attacks on Northern Israel.

MODERN JEWISH AMERICAN LITERATURE:
A BRIEF HISTORY

In the beginning, Jewish writers living in, or having emerged from, the Lower East Side in the 1882–1924 period were immigrants or children of immigrants. English was not their first language. By choosing to write in the language of the United States, they signaled that they were reaching out to the greater public. Indeed, writing in English was a part of their personal Americanization. They prided themselves on their mastery of a language with an enormous number of readers. The opportunities, openness, and freedom of America energized them and encouraged them to actualize their talents. They succeeded in stepping onto a worldwide stage.

But they were still Jews—Lower East Side Jews—even when they some-times tried to disguise that truth by conversion or marriage outside the faith. They wrote for two audiences at the same time: their Jewish readers and the English-speaking community. Which audience was prioritized? That was an individual decision for each of the early Jewish American writers.

The first generation of Jewish American authors, such as Abraham Cahan, Anzia Yezierska, Mary Antin, Rose Cohen, Michael Gold, Daniel Fuchs, and Henry Roth, began the tradition of erudite and popular Jewish American writing. They left a legacy for all Americans—a legacy that now includes the works of Saul Bellow, Paddy Chayefsky, Edward Dahlberg, Babette Deutsch, E. L. Doctorow, Kenneth Fearing, Edna Ferber, Bruce Jay Friedman, Allen Gins-burg, Anthony Hecht, Joseph Heller, Lillian Hellman, Fannie Hurst, David Ignatow, George S. Kaufman, Maxine Kumin, Stanley Kunitz, Tony Kushner, Denise Levertov, Meyer Levin, David Mamet, Norman Mailer, Bernard Malamud, Arthur Miller, Howard Nemerov, Clifford Odets, Tillie Olsen, Cynthia Ozick, Grace Paley, Dorothy Parker, Marge Piercy, Robert Pinsky, Chaim Potok, Charles Reznikoff, Elmer Rice, Adrienne Rich, Thane Rosenbaum, Philip Roth, J. D. Salinger, Budd Schulberg, Karl Shapiro, Irwin Shaw, Neil Simon, Susan

Sontag, Gertrude Stein, Leon Uris, Wendy Wasserstein, Nathanael West, Herman Wouk, Marya Zaturenska, and many others.

Jewish American culture is partly a literary culture that began in a unique neighborhood: the Lower East Side of Manhattan. That literary culture, with its ethnic resonance, welcomed female writers from the beginning. It crossed the traditional dividing line of popular and "high" culture, and it still presents a fresh critique of the American setting. To a certain extent, the reading of Jewish American writers by American Jews has provided a community cohesion that supplements or sometimes replaces the synagogue and the temple. Happily, that culture lives on and flourishes.

It was inevitable that the vibrant early twentieth-century New York City ghetto culture would expand and produce high-quality writing that would catch the attention of the American public, many of whom were very interested in the ethos, values, and lifestyles of those new immigrants who seemed so ambitious, so anxious to feel and be at home, and so filled with energy and drive.

Almost without exception the first generation of Jewish American writers simply presented realistic portrayals—warts and all—of their fellow immigrants or their parents' generation. Later, some other Americans, partial to anti-Semitism, found confirmation of negative stereotypes in the new Jewish American literature. Indeed, some parent-hating or self-hating Jewish American writers of the second or third generation, living now in the bounty of American affluence, consciously reinforced negative stereotypes with satire and a selective realism. For the most part, however, Jewish anti-Semitism was a phenomenon of the Depression and the 1940s, years of a general and strident anti-Semitism in the United States and Europe.

The early Jewish American writers encompassed many themes in their work, some resulting from the experience of immigration and acculturation, others from the household tensions brought about by relocation, poverty, generational conflict, smother love, and patriarchal tyranny. They tried to comprehend, cope with, and accept the merciless capitalistic system into which all were thrust. The Lower East Side workplace was a compactor of workers, mashing former yeshiva students, educated gymnasium graduates, Talmudic sages, homemaking mothers, and unskilled children into a machine that ground out garments, artificial flowers, and cigars. Shockingly for the newly created urban proletariat, the heavy-handed employers were often co-religionists—German Jews whose grandparents had been immigrants in the same neighborhood the Eastern European Jews now inhabited. Or, the new capitalists were recent Eastern European Jews, or their children, who perhaps had a little capital to start with and had quickly learned to exploit the system.

The writers also addressed the question of assimilation, some seeing it as a mixed blessing, others as an unfortunate consequence of coming to America. But when the ultimate results of assimilation were self-hatred and intermarriage, it was always a family tragedy. In almost all the Jewish American writers' literature of the mass immigration period there is a sense that their religion is dying. It slowly vanishes from their texts. Not only do the Orthodox Jewish practices of Eastern Europe not fit into the New World, they seem to make the individual unfit for that world.

In today's Jewish American writing the theme of assimilation has become a minor one as large numbers of American Jews have found spouses and partners from other religions and races without facing calumny and disapproval from the Jewish or the gentile community.

Lastly, anti-Semitism is a theme in the early texts, but, significantly, it is seldom a major one. This seeming de-emphasis on anti-Semitism is not because it was not present in the immigration and post-immigration experiences of Lower East Side Jews, but, alas, because the Eastern European Jews had always lived with it and expected outbreaks of it. Though anti-Semitism had no legal status and was not accompanied by bloody pogroms, racism and class discrimination were part of the American way of life at the turn of the twentieth century.

Early Jewish American fiction is built around a series of quests, symbolic or practical, not the least of which is the desire for physical comfort and material success, which when achieved in early Jewish American fiction is usually accompanied with guilt feelings toward friends and family left behind, as well as the sense of betrayal of the spiritual and humane precepts of Judaism.

Another quest is the archetypal Telemechus theme: searching for and finding the lost father. For the young members or children of the immigrant generation the Jewish father symbolized the controlling religion from which the young strove to escape, but in maturity they came to feel that they had betrayed their religious fathers. They experienced guilt and a sense of structural loss in abandoning the faith of their fathers.

In the end the early Jewish American writers craved recognition from the mainstream critical American world of letters, and they hungered for wide acceptance from the general reading public. Individually their work was often cathartic, an outlet for repressed feelings about parents, siblings, unattainable mates, marital mismatches, and other plagues of the mind. But self-analytic investigation and justification aside, most of all they were literary artists.

The portrait of the gentile world changed when the second generation of Jewish American writers began to publish in the 1940s. That world became less fascinating and less fearful. The Anglo-Saxon way of life with its power, seeming gentility, and exclusivity, which seemed a goal for the immigrant writers, soon appeared more complicated, less worthy of imitation, life-denying, and in decline.

Now East European Jewish life began to seem too distant to be relevant. Jewish American writers remained on the left of the political spectrum. They also rejected some traditional themes in the general mid-twentieth-century American novel such as the machismo of the hero as in Ernest Hemingway and the high-society lifestyle as in F. Scott Fitzgerald. With his first novel, *Dangling Man* (1944), Saul Bellow was instrumental in moving the focus of the Jewish American novel from physical action to the sphere of the often angst-ridden intellect. Norman Mailer's *The Naked and the Dead* (1948) attacked the immorality and the futility of war. Bernard Malamud displayed his compassion for the poor, the underdog, the alienated, the loser, and the schlemiel in such novels as *A New Life* (1961) and the *Fixer* (1966), as well as in his short stories. E. L. Doctorow revealed the cultural diffusion and density of his native city, New York, in such popular novels as *Ragtime* (1975) and *Billy Bathgate* (1989), while concentrating on the relationship between the individual and the state. Most importantly, Philip Roth, who might deny that Jewishness determines his identity, nevertheless has used a vast portion of his great literary talent exploring the tensions, challenges, and contradictions in being an American Jew, especially through his Nathan Zuckerman novels.

ANTI-SEMITISM, THE HOLOCAUST, ZIONISM, AND THE STATE OF ISRAEL

Anti-Semitism

Anti-Semitism is defined as hostility or discrimination toward Jews as a religious or racial group. Historically, it has resulted in persecution, expulsion, and political and economic restrictions. Whereas Jews were largely accepted in American life until decades after the Civil War, it was only when the great Jewish emigration from Central and Eastern Europe to the United States began in the 1880s that bigotry against Jews set in, and anti-Semitism became pervasive.

Negative perceptions of Jews included—and for some Americans still include—such stereotypes as: Jews are clannish, unethical in business, conceited, too powerful, more loyal to Israel than to the United States, and for some ill-informed Christians, Jews are collectively and forever responsible for the death of Jesus.

All Jewish American writers born before 1950 experienced some anti-Semitism in their lives, especially when they were young. One Jewish

American writer, Ben Hecht (1893–1964)—novelist, playwright, and screen writer—said that he had not experienced it in his life, but considering that he spent much of his childhood in the Jewish ghetto in New York City's Lower East Side, and that his early working years were in Chicago, the statement is improbable. Anti-Semitism, in varying degrees, was always an obstacle to overcome by Jewish American writers.

Anti-Semitism in the United States began to decline in the 1960s from its high watermarks in the 1930s and 1940s—when many groups were formed to promote hatred of Jews—due to a better educated public that, in general, grew less prejudiced and more tolerant of minorities.

The Holocaust

The Holocaust is considered to be the greatest crime in the history of the world. It was the systematic slaughter of six million European Jews, including more than two million children, by the Germans under Adolf Hitler from 1933 to 1945. These innocent people were murdered in Germany, Poland, Russia, Hungary, and other European countries when under German occupation and often with the collaboration of fascist, anti-Semitic citizens of the occupied nations. American Jews living in 1945, when the full knowledge of the Holocaust came to world awareness with the surrender of Nazi Germany, suffered shock and agonizing sorrow for the death of European Jewry, the ancestral homeland for many millions of them, and to this day their thoughts and dreams are filled with horror and fear of what racial hatred can lead to in even so-called civilized people.

The word "Holocaust" is from the Greek *holo-*, meaning "whole" or "entire," and *kaustikos*, meaning "burning." Together the meaning is total destruction by fire, or a sacrifice like a burnt offering. The Holocaust, per se, in the 1940s came to specify the murder of six million Jews by the Germans and their allies. It was genocide, a word coined in 1944, signifying the destruction of any ethnic or racial group. Post–World War II genocide has occurred in Cambodia, Rwanda, Iraq, Bosnia, and other places. Sadly, but inevitably, the world has not seen the last of such horror. The Hebrew word for the Holocaust is *Shoah*.

With a few exceptions, most gentile fiction writers have chosen to stay away from the subject, partly out of respect for the dead and the survivors, but mainly because they were unable to cope with a subject and themes where imagination could not encompass the incredibility of the experience. The Holocaust seems to them unsuitable for art because it was just too horrible. Any representation seems to pale before the realities of the event. Post–World

War II Jewish American writing is fully informed by the Holocaust because
that event is the most catastrophic in Jewish history from the fall of Jerusalem
to the Romans in 70 c.e. until now. Jewish American fiction writers who
have addressed the Holocaust in their work include Leslie Epstein, Meyer
Levin, Anne Michaels, Cynthia Ozick, Emily Praeger, Lev Raphael, Norma
Rosen, Thane Rosenbaum, Philip Roth, Susan Schaeffer, Leon Uris, Edward
Wallant, and Herman Wouk.

Even for those who did not personally experience it, the Holocaust has
made it much harder to have faith in God or belief in an intrinsic goodness in
humanity. Furthermore, the question of responsibility will never be answered
satisfactorily because, in the broadest sense, many millions of people world-
wide were involved in the crime—from the local police who rounded up Jews
for shipment to the camps to the world leaders who turned a blind eye to the
slaughter—and the indifferent populations who refused to give sanctuary and
shelter to the helpless and friendless neighbors and fellow citizens: the Jews
of Europe.

The Holocaust had many roots: growing anti-Semitism in late-nineteenth-
century and early twentieth-century Europe, especially in Austria, Poland,
the Russian Empire, and its successor, the Soviet Union; but also in the
Balkan nations, Germany, and even in France, as evidenced by the Dreyfus
Affair (1894–1906).

Fantastic pseudo-scientific racial theories current in the late-nineteenth
century and early twentieth century depicted the Jews as an inferior and
degenerative race that was polluting "pure" European stocks. France and
Great Britain, in their reluctance to stem German rearming in the lull
between the two World Wars, and their subsequent appeasement of Hitler in
the late 1930s, also were a part of the prelude to the Holocaust.

Most significant, however, was the rise of Adolf Hitler (1889–1945) to full
dictatorial power over Germany. Early in 1933 Hitler became the German
Chancellor. He had built the National Socialist Party, the Nazis, on the basis
of his rabid hatred of the Jewish people, first fully evidenced in *Mein Kampf*
(1923), his master plan to make Germany the dominant country in Europe.
Once in power, Hitler opened Germany's first concentration camps, including
Dachau, Buchenwald, and Ravesbrück for women. Also in 1933: the Nazis
decreed that Jews and descendents of Jews were non-Aryan and could no
longer own land; Hitler and the Nazis established the Gestapo, and ordered
the burning of hundreds of thousands of books by Jews, Socialists, and writers
whom the Nazis considered decadent; Hitler announced that the Nazi Party
would be the only German political party; and the Nazis also ordered forced
sterilization of people found to have genetic defects.

The next year Hitler took the title of Führer, as 90 percent of the German electorate approved his usurpation of full and unchallenged power. In 1935 Hitler imposed the infamous Nuremberg Race Laws on German Jews. Jews were stripped of educational and business opportunities and civil rights. In 1938 the Austrian people welcomed Hitler and the German Army as Austria entered a union with Germany. At least 200,000 Austrian Jews fell into Hitler's demonic power. Mauthausen Concentration Camp was constructed. Jews had to register their wealth. A League of Nations conference called by the United States and attended by representatives of 32 countries discussed the Jewish refugee problem, but, cruelly, not a single nation, including the United States, was willing to take in any significant number of Jews. On the night of November 9, 1938, Nazi storm troopers rampaged throughout Germany and destroyed scores of synagogues, and killed hundreds and beat thousands of Jews. The date is forever known as *Kristallnacht*. All Jewish businesses were confiscated, and all Jewish children were banned from schools.

Early in 1939 Germany occupied Czechoslovakia with its population of 350,000 Jews. On September 1, Germany invaded Poland, and World War II commenced. Over two million Polish Jews were now in the power of Hitler and his Jew-hating henchmen. As Poland was conquered, its Jews were ordered into ghettos by railroad stations in order to be ready for further transportation. All adult Jews had to wear a yellow Star of David to mark them and separate them from the rest of the population. Adolf Eichmann, a skilled administrator, rose in the Gestapo hierarchy to take control of Jewish affairs, transportation, and deportation.

In 1940 the Auschwitz Concentration Camp in Poland opened, and Germany began to deport its Jewish population to Poland. The German army conquered Denmark, Norway, France, Belgium, Holland, and Luxembourg. Hungry, Romania, and Slovakia joined the Axis, and 600,000 more Jews were in grave danger. Almost all of Western and Central Europe was in German hands. Jewish ghettos in Kraków, Lodz, and Warsaw, Poland, were sealed off, trapping 700,000 Jews. The next year the Germans occupied Bulgaria, Yugoslavia, and Greece, bringing 200,000 more Jews under Hitler's power. The Germans then invaded the Soviet Union, which had a Jewish population of three million. After the Japanese surprise attack on Pearl Harbor on December 7, 1941, Hitler declared war on the United States, and the German Army began murdering all Jews in occupied Soviet areas.

In 1942 the Wannsee Conference in a Berlin suburb planned the "Final Solution"—the extermination of European Jewry. Gas chambers at various concentration camps became operative, and the camps became extermination camps. Trainloads of money and valuables stolen from Jews were sent back to Germany.

The estimated number of Jews killed by early 1943 was one million. All Gypsies found were also sent to extermination camps. Homosexuals were equally victimized. Ghettos were systematically wiped out. As the Western Allies moved into Italy, the Germans occupied Rome and northern Italy, bringing 35,000 Italian Jews under their control. Fortunately, in Denmark the courageous Resistance transported over 7,000 Jews to safety in neutral Sweden.

In 1944, while the Allied armies had landed in France and were driving toward Germany, and as the Soviet army reached Poland, Hungary, a German ally, was fully occupied by the Germans, who, under Adolf Eichmann, rounded up Hungarian Jews and shipped almost 400,000 to their death at Auschwitz. The brave Swedish diplomat Raoul Wallenberg saved some 33,000 Hungarian Jews by issuing diplomatic papers protecting them. In Amsterdam, Anne Frank and her family were captured and transported to Auschwitz where she died. The Warsaw Ghetto rose up in a third and final battle against the Germans. After weeks of resistance, when the last Jews were killed, the Germans demolished the ghetto. Soon the Soviet army began liberating concentration camps. As the terrible year ended, the death camps were being destroyed by the retreating Germans.

In 1945 Auschwitz, where two million Jews and other Poles were murdered, was liberated by the Soviet army. The Western Allies liberated Buchenwald, Bergen-Belsen, and Dachau. Hitler committed suicide in a Berlin bunker as the Soviet army closed in, and Germany surrendered unconditionally to the Allies on May 7, 1945.

The Holocaust was over. Approximately six million Jewish children, women, and men, had been murdered by the Germans and their Austrian, Polish, French, Hungarian, Romanian, Slovakian, Bulgarian, Lithuanian, Estonian, and Latvian accomplices.

The Holocaust cannot even be called a tragedy in the technical Aristotelian sense in which a tragic hero falls because of his or her own actions, a tragic flaw, or fate. The Jews were simply trapped and helpless human beings. They were not flawed tragic figures. Nothing in their individual characters mattered. They might as well have been engulfed in a natural disaster like a tsunami for all they could have done to prevent their fate. Today, humanity mourns its inestimable loss. Nazi Germany essentially destroyed the European Jewish community and the Jewish gene pool that had given the world a store of genius and creativity that made it a better place for all of us to live in.

Zionism

Zionism originated as a late-nineteenth-century nationalist movement to establish a Jewish homeland in Palestine, the land of the Biblical ancestors of the Jewish people. It was in part a reaction to the pogroms in czarist Russia and the vilification of Jews in France during and after the previously mentioned Dreyfus Affair. The basic plan was to promote agricultural settlements in the Turkish-controlled territory. In 1897 Theodor Herzl (1860–1904), a Viennese journalist, founded the First Zionist Congress, which advocated working for a homeland for the nation-less Jewish people. The movement was given impetus by the British Government in the Balfour Declaration of World War I (1917), which supported a Jewish homeland in Palestine. After World War II ended in 1945, many Holocaust survivors made their way to Palestine where they helped to establish the State of Israel in 1948.

Today, people who support Israel in and outside of the state are often referred to as Zionists. The term is used as a pejorative by Islamic terrorists and neo-fascists.

The State of Israel

After World War I (1914–1918), Great Britain was given control of Palestine as a mandate of the League of Nations. Jewish land purchases and an influx of Holocaust survivors after 1945 swelled the Jewish population of the mandate causing resentment, hostility, and violence on the part of the Arab population of Palestine. When the United Nations partitioned Palestine into a Jewish and an Arab state in 1947, the Jewish population accepted the dictum and established their state, but the Arab population supported by all the Arab nations of the Middle East made war on the Jews and were defeated after Israel declared its independence in 1948.

The new State of Israel engaged successfully in major conflicts with the intransigent neighboring Arab nations in 1956, 1967, and 1973. At this writing, Arab-Israeli conflict has again broken out. From 1947 to the present most Jewish American writers have been supporters of Israel even when they sometimes disagreed with specific Israeli actions.

1

Abraham Cahan
The Rise of David Levinsky
(1917)

In 1896 D. Appleton and Company of New York published Abraham Cahan's short novel, *Yekl: A Tale of the New York Ghetto*, and a path was opened for Jewish American Literature. William Dean Howells, a leading novelist and major critic of American literature at the time, and Cahan's mentor, too, hailed Cahan as a new master of literary realism. But writing fiction in English was only a small part of Cahan's long life. He was a great socialist leader of East Side Jewry, a major spokesperson for the American Jewish community, and the founder and for decades the editor-in-chief of the *Jewish Daily Forward*, the most important Jewish newspaper in America.

BIOGRAPHICAL CONTEXT

Abraham Cahan was born in 1860 in Podberezy, near Vilna, Lithuania, then within the Russian Empire. When he was five years old his Orthodox Jewish family moved to Vilna, now Vilnius, in which a large, intellectual, and politically active Jewish population lived, and where his parents expected that Abraham would eventually become a rabbi. Nevertheless, Cahan's basic education was in Russian. He studied at the Teachers' Institute in Vilna from 1877 to 1881 and was certified to teach in Jewish schools where Russian was the language of instruction. Cahan soon became active in radical socialist politics, and he fled possible prosecution after the assassination of Czar Alexander II in 1881, an event immediately followed by widespread and devastating government-supported pogroms.

Cahan arrived in New York City in 1882 penniless and in need of a job. Like tens of thousands of other immigrant Jews, he found employment in the cigar factories while he learned the language of his new country. In a year he began publishing newspaper articles in English. His first article, an 1883 piece in the *New York World*, attacked Imperial Russia. An ardent socialist, Cahan championed labor and helped to organize unions.

Cahan was a humanist and an atheist. He loved the Jewish people, and he strove to show the world how rich Jewish culture was, and how the Jewish people shared the hopes and aspirations, the needs and the gifts, the compassion and the love of life, of all humanity.

In 1897 Cahan founded the Yiddish-language *Jewish Daily Forward*. Initially it floundered, and Cahan left it only to return in 1903 as the managing editor who led the *Forward* in its successful drive to become the largest circulation Jewish newspaper in America. Cahan made sure that the newspaper devoted much of its space to the arts. He was responsible for introducing the fiction of Nobel Prize-winning Isaac Bashevis Singer, Israel Joshua Singer (Isaac's older brother), and Sholem Asch to the Yiddish-reading public. Cahan's Socialism never evolved into Communism. Having welcomed the Russian Revolution in 1917, by 1921 Cahan realized that the Revolution had been diverted from true Socialism, and that Bolshevism presented as despotic a threat to democracy as had Russian Imperialism.

Cahan's wife, Anna Bronstein Cahan, a well-educated intellectual from Kiev whom he married in 1886, guided him toward the writing of fiction. His first published story, "A Providential Match," was written in Yiddish. Later he translated it into English, and it appeared in *The Imported Bridegroom and Other Stories of the New York Ghetto* (1898). This collection followed the first important work of Jewish American fiction, Cahan's *Yekl: A Tale of the New York Ghetto* (1896), the story of an immigrant man's loss of his loving family because of the temptations of American life.

The two great influences on Cahan's fiction were the naturalism of American writers such as Stephen Crane, Upton Sinclair, and Frank Norris, and the European naturalism of Émile Zola, Israel Zangwell, and Maxim Gorky. Like each of these writers, Cahan exposed a part of humanity and a way of life few readers knew anything about, for a basic purpose behind naturalism was to change the perceptions of poor urban life in the minds of middle- and upper-class readers.

From 1899 to 1901 Cahan published six more stories in *Cosmopolitan*, *Scribner's*, *Century*, and *Atlantic Monthly*. In all of his short stories, Cahan is skillful in creating believable characters and in setting a Jewish ghetto scene. He also moralizes against the material temptations of America, as well as the greed of employers and some workers.

In 1905 Cahan turned to the novel form when he published *The White Terror and the Red*, a story about revolutionary activity in Russia prior to the assassination of Czar Alexander II in 1881, the event that triggered the massive pogroms that provoked hundreds of thousands of Eastern European Jews to leave their ancestral homes for America. The story centers on the love of a Russian prince and a young Jewish woman. They are revolutionaries, and before they can be married, they are captured, imprisoned, and are waiting for execution when the novel ends.

Although Cahan knew his subject well, *The White Terror and the Red* was not a successful novel. It is marred by Cahan's attempt to teach history as well as write fiction. Fortunately, Cahan was not discouraged. He now had the experience of writing a long and involved narrative. This served him well in his last and most brilliant work of fiction, *The Rise of David Levinsky*.

The publication history of *The Rise of David Levinsky* began with its four-part 1913 serialization in *McClure Magazine*. The intent was to show how a Jewish immigrant might rise from abject poverty to great wealth. The key was success in the garment industry. The industry had been controlled largely by German American Jews who had been in New York for one or two generations. Although most of the new immigrants in the industry worked as machine operators, some saved money and set up competing factories that took much of the trade away from their coreligionists.

As a well-educated new American, Cahan could see the contemporary scene from a Jewish immigrant and an American establishment viewpoint. He saw the shortcomings of some of his coreligionists at the same time that he valorized the collective achievement of entrepreneurial Eastern European Jewish immigrants who so quickly grasped the Protestant work ethic and the American dream of material success. Still, it took a long time for Cahan's readers, both Jew and gentile, to come to appreciate Cahan's truthful unveiling of Jewish drive. Some wrongly felt that in his depiction of some unprincipled business practices by individual Jews in *The Rise of David Levinsky*, Cahan was reinforcing negative stereotypes and evidencing a degree of Jewish self-hatred. The charge was unfair. David Levinsky is a true-to-life character. He has good and bad qualities. He is as much to be pitied as he is to be disliked. The final version of *The Rise of David Levinsky* (1917) quickly became the first classic of Jewish American literature. It is also a major document in American social history.

Between 1926 and 1931 Cahan wrote his five-volume autobiography in Yiddish. The first two volumes, his life to 1914, were translated and published in English as *The Education of Abraham Cahan* (1969). Cahan worked on the "Forward" almost to his death in 1951. Sadly, he had lived to see the extermination of the Jewish population of Europe and the demise of the language he loved most of all, Yiddish.

PLOT DEVELOPMENT

David Levinsky, the protagonist in *The Rise of David Levinsky*, is the person Cahan could have become if he had left Vilna as a teenager. Writing out of his Russian socialist perspective, he infused the character of the rising industrialist with his own fascination with the pitfalls and the possibilities of American life.

The 528-page novel is divided into 14 books. The first four are set in the town of Antomir in Russia. David's father died before the child was three years old, and David and his impoverished, overprotective, Orthodox Jewish mother live in a corner of a cellar. She scrapes together funds to give David some schooling, and he receives an Orthodox Jewish education. In a Talmudic seminary he makes a close friend, Naphtali, a gentle youth who eventually confesses that he does not believe in God. Mrs. Levinsky is proud that her son is a good student. But David's mind is not always on his studies. He thinks of women, and he dwells on his hatred for a competing scholar. One day David returns home having been harassed and beaten by gentiles. His fearless mother rushes out to attack his tormentors. Struck in the head, she is carried home to die.

David is now hungry and reliant on charity. A pious rich woman gives him meals regularly, but David has lost interest in his studies. He contemplates emigration to America. However, he meets Matilda, the attractive, divorced "modern" daughter of the rich woman. She teases the yeshiva student and urges him to obtain a real education. David falls in love with the older woman. They hug and kiss a lot, and Matilda is willing to introduce him to sex, but he is so naïve as not to understand when she signals receptivity. Matilda quickly tires of immature David, but generously offers to obtain money for his passage to America. Although he is broken-hearted and would like to stay with her, he accepts the offer.

In books five through eight, Cahan delineates, through Levinsky's first experiences in New York City, the struggles of a friendless Jewish immigrant without sellable skills, without English, and without relatives or friends in the city. Fortunately, a kind man he meets in a synagogue helps Levinsky, but his religion quickly leaves him. Needing to earn money, he becomes a peddler. Needing sexual relief, he goes to prostitutes. Homesick, he also longs for Matilda. Studying English in night school, he makes friends with his teacher, Mr. Bender, who eventually will become a loyal employee of Levinsky.

Instead of devoting himself entirely to peddling, in order to educate himself Levinsky becomes an avid reader of English novelists such as Charles Dickens. A chance East Side meeting with Gittleson, a tailor he first became acquainted with aboard the immigrant ship, sends Levinsky into the garment industry as an apprentice sewing machine operator, even though his real wish is to study at City College. At work he meets and proposes marriage to Gussie, a fellow worker, hoping that she will support him while he goes to college, but she will not be used that way.

Having been humiliated at work by an overbearing boss, Levinsky determines to go into business for himself. Thoughts of higher education evaporate. Meeting a clothing designer named Chaikin, and scraping together capital and credit by whatever means possible, Levinsky and Chaikin start a business, but it almost immediately fails due to bad luck.

In book nine David falls in love for the second time. Max Margolis, a friend, invites him home to meet his wife, Dora, and his young daughter, Lucy. Meanwhile, another friend lends him money, and an unexpected check for back goods arrives. Levinsky has his second chance. He becomes a boarder in the Margolis household, and he and Dora fall in love and have an affair. The young mother is guilt-ridden by what she has given in to. Levinsky urges Dora to divorce her husband and marry him. Because of her child, Dora refuses, and David moves out.

Levinsky is deeply saddened, but business is great. He has nonunion workers earning less than union scale and that gives him an advantage over the union shops. He has become the same kind of boss he once hated. Reading Charles Darwin's *The Origin of the Species* and Herbert Spencer, the social Darwinist, Levinsky becomes convinced that he is succeeding because he is one of the fittest and they always come out on top.

In the tenth book, we learn of Levinsky's growing success as a manufacturer and his belief that he needs—indeed deserves—a wife. In the eleventh through thirteenth books, Levinsky's personal and social life are emphasized. Matilda, married to a Russian, has come to New York to lecture at Cooper Union on behalf of political prisoners in Russia. When Levinsky goes to the hall to meet her, she sees an overdressed capitalist, and she spurns him. He in turn becomes truly reactionary, hardening his heart against workers and radicals.

At the age of 40 Levinsky courts and proposes marriage to Fanny, the daughter of a rich businessman who is also a Talmudist. Levinsky is not in love with Fanny, but he believes she would be an appropriate wife for him. Just before the marriage he stops off at a Catskill resort where he sees and falls immediately in love with Anna Tevkin, the daughter of a Hebrew poet whose published love letters to his wife once sexually aroused David and his friend Naphtali in Antomir. Levinsky is besotted with passion, but Anna does not care for him at all. Nevertheless, he breaks his engagement and pursues Anna by courting her father, now a real estate broker in New York City, and inveigling himself into the artistic and radical Tevkin family. Finally, he asks Anna to marry him and she emphatically turns him down. Levinsky is devastated. He has lost the greatest love of his life.

The fourteenth book has Levinsky turning entirely to business. His fortune multiplies. He meets Matilda again, and this time they are cordial with each other, but meeting old friends and loves only increases Levinsky's loneliness. He comes close to marrying an intelligent and kind gentile widow, but in feeling out the situation he realizes that the cultural gulf between them is too great. Also, as he begins to hint at a lasting relationship, she remains clearly noncommittal.

So David Levinsky, in the end, finds some solace in reading great literature. If he can't live life in the flesh, he will live it in the book. Chained to the pull of his early upbringing and the memory of the poverty of his youth, he remains uneasy with his wealth. All he can do is make money.

CHARACTER DEVELOPMENT

For Cahan, plot evolves from character, and character is determined by environment. The environments of Levinsky's early life, a Russian town rife with poverty and anti-Semitism, and the Lower East Side at its most crowded and competitive moment, make for the barbed nature of his character. Levinsky is not a likable protagonist. He let his widowed mother fight his battle for him, and she was killed in the process. He uses her sacrifice to obtain sympathy and advantages from those who feel sorry for an orphan. In America he tries hard to Americanize, to fit in, but he never quite succeeds. He has the clothes but not the class. He has abandoned his religion, education, and culture to run after money. He uses people and then discards them when they are no longer of use to him. His business practices, personifying social Darwinism, are excessively aggressive and sometimes treacherous. He exploits his workers. He is disloyal. He betrays a friend by making love to the man's wife. Generally, he is manipulative with women. His egoism is off-putting, and he is excessively self-satisfied.

Yet, we also feel sorry for this melancholy, alienated, deracinated immigrant. It's a cliché, of course, but Levinsky never learns that happiness can't really be bought. He is fated never to be happy or content.

In *The Rise of David Levinsky*, Abraham Cahan created one of the greatest characters of Jewish American fiction. David Levinsky may not quite be a titan of industry, but he is a titan of the late-nineteenth- to early-twentieth-century school of American literary realism.

The most important people in Levinsky's fascinating life are the women he loves. All of them are finely drawn by Cahan. They stand out among the host of interesting characters in the novel, mainly because they are so important to the development of Levinsky's character, or lack of it.

Levinsky's mother, the impoverished widow in Antomir, is overly protective of her son. She is a strong, outspoken person, hardened by adversity. Her maternal instinct is fierce. When her 18-year-old son is beaten by anti-Semitic thugs, in a rage she storms out of their hovel to take revenge, and she is rewarded by being beaten to death. But even in death she serves her son, as Levinsky unscrupulously uses his mother's murder to evoke sympathy from those willing to help the orphan with charity.

Matilda Minsker, the young, sexy, Russian-educated, divorced Jewish woman, a few years older than Levinsky, who attempts to seduce the poor yeshiva boy, is frustrated because the virginal youth does not know what to do, and so she decides to get rid of him by providing money to get him to America. Matilda represents sexual temptation.

Dora, the wife of Max Margolis, one of Levinsky's few Lower East Side friends, is not happy with her verbose and crude husband. She is attractive. She has a beautiful daughter. Levinsky falls in love with her and with the possibility of a warm and happy home if he could convince her to divorce Max. Initially, she resists Levinsky, partly because she is honest and partly because of her concern for her daughter. Finally, Levinsky seduces her. But Dora is stricken with guilt, and her husband is morbidly suspicious.

Although Levinsky loves Dora, and especially would like to continue their sexual relationship, he does not reveal the affair to Dora's husband in order to provoke a divorce that would allow him to marry Dora. It seems a torrid affair was what Levinsky really desired. Dora, however, is crushed, and she will live out a loveless marriage in despair. As time goes by, Levinsky mourns for his lost love and the happiness he thinks he could have had with the warm and loving Dora.

Fanny Kaplin, an attractive, self-centered, American-born and educated girl in her early twenties, is the trophy the 40-year-old industrialist picks for a bride, when, bored with making money, he at last decides to marry. Passively, Fanny accepts an engagement. Levinsky is rich, and her parents eagerly approve. It is not a love match. When Levinsky meets Anna Tevlin he unabashedly breaks off his engagement and pays compensation. The implication is that Fanny is not unhappy with the outcome, and the reader feels she is better off not becoming Levinsky's wife.

Anna Tevlin is an American-educated young woman, the daughter of a Yiddish poet who is struggling to make a living for his family by working as a real estate broker. Levinsky is not only passionately drawn to Anna, he also finds something finely spiritual in her. Alas, she, an ardent socialist, is not at all interested in this older bourgeois, whom she sees as a crude exploiter of workers. Levinsky ingratiates himself with Anna's father by purchasing some real estate from him, but when he proposes to Anna, she is horrified, and she bluntly turns him down. Levinsky is crushed. Neither his ardor nor his money could win or buy the love of a sensitive woman of integrity. In the end, Levinsky will not marry, nor will he ever love again.

THEMES

The struggle of Ghetto life is a major theme in *The Rise of David Levinsky*. Indeed, late-nineteenth- and early-twentieth-century Jewish New York City looms darkly over this realistic novel. Cahan vividly portrays the overcrowded flats; the restless, teeming streets; the soul-destroying sweatshops; the nascent and flamboyant Yiddish theater; the noisy, crowded synagogues; and the busy cafés with their forever talking, arguing, and debating poets and intellectuals. The vastness of the metropolis makes its inhabitants painfully more separated from each other than they would be in a less populated environment. Consequently, Cahan the moralist implies that people must strive to be more caring and responsible for each other.

The theme of the limitations of money is a structural element in the novel. Cahan saw a kind of tragedy in the pursuit of wealth. Levinsky and, by extension, the aggressive new rich fell as they rose. The Faustian bargain was to exchange their soul for gold. The constant attention to making more money, the loss of friendships on the way up, the jettisoning of religion, the betrayal of comrades and loved ones, the fading interest in things cultural, and the suspicion of others, slowly dissolve integrity and character. In that *The Rise of David Levinsky* is about "making it," it is an American book. In that it is about the exploitation of workers and the selfish manipulation of the means of production, it is a socialist book. In that it is about the waste of an intelligent person and the loss of a soul, it is a Jewish book.

NARRATIVE STYLE

The Rise of David Levinsky is the first-person flashback of a millionaire clothing manufacturer. The year is 1913 and Levinsky is 52 years old—interestingly, about the same age as Cahan—as he begins to relate the facts of his life from his childhood in Russia to the present day. The writing style is the American plain style of William Dean Howells and his contemporaries. The prose is sparse and precise. Cahan set out to exhaust the milieu of the Jewish immigrant from the last decades of the nineteenth century through the first decade of the twentieth.

Unlike later Jewish American writers such as Anzia Yezierska, Michael Gold, and Henry Roth, Cahan implants absolutely no Yiddish flavor or tone in *The Rise of David Levinsky*. There is no attempt at dialect. Cahan respects English, and he respects the immigrant. Furthermore, it seems apparent that the reader Cahan had in mind was an American-born gentile. Cahan assumed correctly that the American establishment could make life easier for the Jewish immigrant, and would do so if they recognized the intelligence, humanity, and dignity of these fellow human beings. Thus, Cahan's characters speak English clearly and well, and the novel is accessible.

Cahan's realism is different from much of the genre in that it is devoid of sensationalism and violence. His style is close to the naturalistic novels of Frank Norris and Theodore Dreiser. Cahan is a master of description. The reader can almost smell the filth-strewn streets of the overcrowded ghetto, taste the food that is eaten, and easily visualize the many types of people who inhabit Levinsky's world. Also, he skillfully evokes the geography of turn-of-the-twentieth-century New York City, and through his power of recollection he recreates a Russian Jewish shtetl (village or small town), Antomir, Levinsky's birthplace.

Additionally, Cahan reifies pre-Holocaust Eastern European Jewish life. Perhaps out of nostalgia, Cahan is somewhat kinder to the European location of the novel than to many locales in America. One outstanding example is the Catskill summer resort marriage market, where Levinsky goes to contemplate his forthcoming, but never actuated, marriage to Fanny, and where he sees Anna, the great passion of his life. There he finds crass young women and fortune-seeking young men attempting to best each other. There young women are peddled on their looks and their father's money—not necessarily in that order. The new Americans, those now affluent, are loud, gormandizing, nouveau riche. Once hungry in childhood, they cannot get too much to eat and bolt their food down, while showing off their status by overdressing and wearing ostentatious jewelry.

HISTORICAL CONTEXT

In *The Rise of David Levinsky*, Cahan was not only writing fiction, he was recording a chapter in American economic history. The era was that of the muckrakers in American literature, when writers like Upton Sinclair exposed the social Darwinism of the wealthy who thought that their wealth was proof of their superiority—they were the "fittest" in the unregulated jungle called business. Cahan, like the muckrakers—a title coined by President Theodore Roosevelt in 1906—strove to expose the social, economic, and political corruption of industrial life in the United States.

Cahan was never in love with money. It was easy, therefore, for him to show how the capitalistic pursuit of wealth was morally debasing and detrimental to happiness. This is what Cahan's mentor William Dean Howells had established in his famous novel *The Rise of Silas Lapham* (1885), the book that strongly influenced *The Rise of David Levinsky*. Paradoxically, the unsentimental Cahan knew that developing industries, first run by exploiters, eventually could bring better wages and a higher standard of living for workers. But workers needed the support of honest lawmakers and the strength of unions in order to achieve economic justice through collective bargaining.

As Adam Smith proposed in the eighteenth century, greed can eventually serve the common good, but not by letting that greed run rampant without social restraint. Cahan seems intuitively to have understood early-twentieth-century American business, capital formation, and power structure better than many social scientists and critics of his time, and he was not scornful of enterprise.

SUGGESTED READINGS

Primary Sources

Cahan, Abraham. *The Education of Abraham Cahan*. Philadelphia: Jewish Publication Society of America, 1969.
———. *The Rise of David Levinsky*. New York: Penguin, 1993.

Secondary Sources

Chametzky, Jules. *From the Ghetto: The Fiction of Abraham Cahan*. Amherst: University of Massachusetts Press, 1977.
Marovitz, Sanford E. *Abraham Cahan*. New York: Twayne, 1996.

2

Anzia Yezierska
Bread Givers
(1925)

Of the first generation of Jewish American writers who were born in Eastern Europe or on the Lower East Side, Anzia Yezierska was the leading female novelist and short-story writer. In *Bread Givers*, she portrays the Lower East Side ghetto existence from a poor woman's perspective. She exults in the possibilities of life in America, but she laments the loss of family cohesion, religious observance, and traditional Jewish values that came with deracination and the pursuit of money. Yezierska was a fiery woman, grabbing with both hands all the experience and opportunity she could, as she demanded recognition of her talent and individuality. She fervently wanted to be seen, heard, and read as one of a kind. She was a whirlwind and a dynamo, and *Bread Givers* exemplifies all the ambition and striving of an immigrant woman determined to succeed in America.

BIOGRAPHICAL CONTEXT

Anzia Yezierska was born in a shtetl mud hut in Plotz, Russian Poland, in 1880. She was the youngest daughter of a religious father, Bernard Yezierska, and Pearl Yezierska, a hard-working, passive mother who was the mainstay of the family. When Anzia was 15, the family, dreaming of wealth in America, migrated to the Lower East Side, where they were only a little better off than they were in Europe. On arrival in New York City, the family took or was given the name Mayer, and Anzia was Hattie Mayer until 1910.

Yezierska's sisters went to work in sweatshops to help support their studious, religious father and their housewife mother. Her brothers went to school and soon left the ghetto, abandoning the family. Anzia, the youngest and most sensitive child, was put to work as an exploited live-in maid. Quitting that demeaning job, and having learned enough English, she found more independent employment sewing in a sweatshop. The workday was long so she strove to improve her English in night school. At 19 she was living on her own, an unusual status for a young Jewish immigrant woman.

Anzia was fractious, sharp-tongued, rebellious, loud, and unpleasant, especially to men. But she was intelligent and passionate, as well as determined to break out of the life of a wage slave.

Impressed with her intelligence and drive, Yezierska's night school teacher encouraged her to obtain further education. Living on her savings, she studied for a year at New York City Normal College. Then she obtained a four-year scholarship to Columbia University Teachers College to learn to teach domestic science to children. Granted a degree and a teaching certificate in 1904, she found employment instructing young Lower East Side girls to cook, clean, and sew. But, disliking teaching and her superiors, she quickly abandoned the profession. Yezierska then decided on a career in the theater and won a scholarship to the prestigious American Academy of Dramatic Arts. Nothing came of that ambition, and she briefly returned to teaching.

Meanwhile Yezierska had made two marriages, one in 1910 with Jacob Gordon, a German Jewish lawyer, that ended in an annulment after six months. The second—a religious ceremony only—in 1911 was to Arnold Levitas, a German Jewish businessman and later a teacher, with whom she had a daughter. But that marriage was not a happy one either. Yezierska hated the role of housewife even though she taught domestic science—or maybe because she did. She also cared little for maternal duties.

In 1913 Yezierska, who had written some verse, began to write fiction. In 1916 she left her husband and, with her consent, Arnold Levitas took custody of their child. Now Yezierska could devote more time to her literary pursuits. Meanwhile, in 1915 her first story, "Free Vacation House," a powerful attack on the arrogance and condescension of settlement workers, was published in *Forum*. Other stories appeared. She quickly learned that life on the Lower East Side was hers to mine.

Seeking to get permission to audit a seminar in social and political thought at Columbia in 1917, Yezierska met the instructor, the distinguished educator and philosopher John Dewey. A relationship developed between them. She was 37; he was 58 and married. She became his research assistant, translator of Yiddish, and lover, while they worked together on a project in Philadelphia. Dewey wrote many love poems to her, but the affair only lasted a year. Much later, Yezierska fictionalized the relationship in *All I Could Never Be* (1932).

In 1919 Yezierska's short story "The Fat of the Land," which had appeared in a magazine in 1918, was named the Best Short Story of 1919 and published in the anthology *The Best Short Stories* (1920). The volume was even dedicated to Yezierska. "The Fat of the Land" is the tale of an elderly East Side Jewish mother of successful children who is unable to live in the fancy uptown apartment house in which her children had warehoused her. She must find her way back to the Lower East Side where she could be comfortable.

As a result of the award, in 1920 Houghton Mifflin published a collection of Yezierska's ghetto stories as *Hungry Hearts*. The Jewish women in her stories— all hungry hearts—were not only hungry for food; they were hungry for love. Yezierska had arrived on the New York literary scene and had become a 1920s celebrity. The film producer Samuel Goldwyn, himself an immigrant Jew from Russian Poland, was impressed by the boldness and intensity of the stories. He purchased the film rights, and Anzia went to Hollywood where she was simultaneously bedazzled and lonely. She felt out of place. The movie *Hungry Hearts*, bearing only a general resemblance to the stories, appeared in 1922. She received a payment of $10,000 and believed she was rich. Later she would receive $15,000 for the film rights to *Salome of the Tenements*. Having realized that she could not write in the glitter of Hollywood, Yezierska returned to her New York City roots.

Salome of the Tenements was published in 1923. Yezierska found the inspiration for this novel in the romance and subsequent marriage in 1905 of her friend Rose Pastor, a fiery Jewish socialist orator, and a millionaire upper-class Protestant, James Phelps Graham Stokes, who worked on the Lower East Side in a settlement house funded by his family. In Anzia's story, Sonya, a female reporter for the *Ghetto News*, is in love with a well-known American philanthropist, and is determined to marry him. She borrows a large sum of money for clothes and furniture to impress him. She succeeds, and they marry. But when the creditor wants his money, she has to pawn her engagement ring. Full of guilt she leaves her husband and eventually opens a not-for-profit dress shop on the Lower East Side in which she helps immigrant women obtain beautiful clothes to make their lives more pleasurable and improve their taste. Helping other women, the penitent Sonya is at last content.

More Yezierska stories were collected in *Children of Loneliness* (1923). Yezierska's narrative skills generally increased with each novel or collection of stories, at least until Yezierska's masterpiece, *Bread Givers* (1925), the story of an immigrant girl's maturation and struggle for independence.

Arrogant Beggar (1927) is based on Yezierska's experiences about the time she was studying domestic science at Columbia Teachers' College. It is the story of a young immigrant girl who works for a socialite and falls in love with her son. The socialite exploits the poor girl, who leaves the house to return to the Lower East Side. She is followed by the son, who proposes marriage. She refuses, and finally finds happiness married to a concert pianist. They will be happy in the nonmaterialist life they'll live together.

All I Could Never Be (1932) harks back to Yezierska's affair with John Dewey. The protagonist, Fanya, an individualist with a passion for social justice, meets a distinguished elderly professor. They become close. Moved by her intensity and lust for life's experiences, he falls in love with Fanya. But when he takes the liberty of kissing her, his romantic image crumbles, she rejects him, and he turns cold. Fanya is now fully disillusioned with life. Ten years later she meets a poor, immigrant artist and finds happiness with him.

With the advent of the Great Depression in 1929, Yezierska's talent seemed to fade away. Her fall in popularity, however, was due in part to the reading public's declining interest in stories of immigrant hardships early in the century, when there were so many contemporary tales of suffering in the cities and countryside. Also, Yezierska seemed to have mined out the thematic vein of her writing. The stories of an immigrant girl struggling to become a person seemed repetitive.

Publishing was hard hit in the Depression. Yezierska's royalties dried up. The Stock Market Crash destroyed her investments. She got some work with the WPA Writers' Project. She moved to a town in New Hampshire, but she couldn't write there; she needed the stimulus of New York City.

Yezierska's last long work was her fictionalized autobiography *Red Ribbon on a White Horse* (1950), which, despite an introduction by W. H. Auden, received little critical attention. The main impression received from the book is that Yezierska was never content with her life. She faded to obscurity even as she kept on writing. She published her last story, "Take Up Your Bed and Walk," in the *Chicago Jewish Forum* in 1969. After her death in 1970 she was rediscovered by the women's movement, and her early work found resonance in the feminist struggle for equality.

Yezierska's major achievement is that she shows the difficult life led by Jewish immigrant women who came to America with hopes for love, respect, individual identity, and economic independence, sometimes only to have those hopes turn into dreams deferred. She did this while brilliantly recreating in words the noises, smells, dirt, crush, and grinding poverty of the ghetto.

PLOT DEVELOPMENT

The plot of *Bread Givers* is rich and satisfying. This paradigmatic novel of immigrant life is set in the tenements on the Lower East Side at the beginning of the twentieth century. The Smolinsky family are Polish-Jewish immigrants. Sara Smolinsky, the heroine, takes on her selfish, mean, domineering father, Reb Smolinsky, who continually bullies his wife, Rifkeh, and four daughters, denigrates women in general, and insists on total obedience from his wife and children to his will and whims. Reb Smolinsky, however, does no work. His excuse for not providing for his family is that he is doing God's work by reading the Torah and studying the Talmud. He is continually preaching to his family. He has reserved an entire room in the small, crowded tenement flat for his study.

Reb Smolinsky feels that he is cursed because he only has daughters, and he blames his wife for that. One by one, he causes his three older daughters to make bad marriages. Bessie, the eldest, is a good-hearted garment industry worker who gives all her wages to the family. She is courted by an up-and-coming garment industry worker, whom she cares for. However, Smolinsky tries to obtain a reverse dowry from the suitor, because if Bessie marries, he will lose her income. The suitor thinks Smolinsky is mad, and he gives up on Bessie. She is forced to marry a widowed fish seller with six children. He is 30 years older than poor Bessie, and she despises him. Her life turns into pure drudgery as she works in the fish store and raises the troublesome children of another woman.

Mashah is the beautiful daughter. She falls in love with a concert pianist, whose wealthy father—another patriarch—discourages the marriage. But it is Smolinsky who terminates the relationship, because he is insulted by the rich man's scorn. His excuse is that the pianist does not keep the Sabbath. Smolinsky then forces the wounded Mashah to marry a man he thinks is a wealthy diamond merchant, but he is only a salesman, and he loses his job. Then he works as a shoe salesman. Indifferent to the children, he spends the food money on clothes for himself and restaurant meals, and he is abusive to Mashah. Her life will always be miserable.

Fania is in love with a poet. Smolinsky insults him and drives him away. He has a wealthy Los Angeles clothes buyer lined up for Fania. Like her older sisters, she accepts a loveless match just to get out of the hellish home they are trapped in. Fania's husband turns out to be a compulsive gambler, and though she lives in material comfort, she is never to be happy because her husband's addiction leaves her lonely and unsatisfied.

Sara, the narrator and heroine, is the daughter who fights back. At age 10 she goes on the street to sell herring for the family. When she is old enough to work in a paper box factory, her father takes all her wages, and she is without a warm coat in the winter. Finally, Reb Smolinsky has saved some money, because the family has taken in boarders. Although he failed in business in Europe, Smolinsky buys a grocery store in Elizabeth, New Jersey. He thinks he has found a good bargain, because the store is supposedly well stocked. But there is no stock. He has been swindled. When he abuses Sara for giving a customer two cents credit, she confronts Smolinsky with his foolishness, hypocrisy, and cruelty, and runs away.

Back on the Lower East Side, Sara finds a hovel to live in, obtains sweat-shop work in the daytime, and goes to night school to prepare for higher edu-cation. She is almost 21 when she enrolls in an out-of-town college, which she works her way through in a laundry. At commencement she wins a $1,000 prize for an essay, and she returns to New York City just as her mother is dying and her father is ready to marry the upstairs widow, who is only after the insurance money that will come with Rifkeh's death. Sara is furious with Smolinsky's quick remarriage. But the old tyrant is punished by the nastiness and greed of his new wife. It is just what Smolinsky deserves. Eventually, the new Mrs. Smolinsky drives Reb Smolinsky out on the streets peddling chew-ing gum.

When Sara, approaching 30—a successful elementary schoolteacher in courtship with Hugo Seelig, her principal—sees what has happened to her father, she brings him to live with her and Hugo whom presumably—although it is never stated—she has married. Now Reb Smolinsky can have his reli-gious books to read in peace and end his life in comfort. Sara has even come to respect his dignity and his religiousness.

In *Bread Givers*, Yezierska wars on the restrictions and built-in misogyny of Orthodox Judaism. She demands that immigrant women be valued for qualities outside of the domestic sphere, and that they value themselves for what they can accomplish in education, the arts, politics, and business, the so-called men's spheres.

CHARACTER DEVELOPMENT

Anzia Yezierska brilliantly created the most vivid female character in early Jewish American fiction: Sara Smolinsky, a tough and feisty individual who at the age of 10 helps her impoverished family by selling herring on the street, and who loves her mother and her sisters, but, as she matures, she eschews their slavish adherence to their father's dictatorial will. Sara is a prodigal daughter, a proto-feminist, who strikes off on her own, lives in poverty while in night school, goes away to college, becomes a teacher, and marries her principal, but in the end, she returns to her old father, makes peace with him, brings him home, and cares for him.

Sara's feminist credentials are clear when she fights her father for the right of her sisters to marry men of their choice. When in a cafeteria line she is not given any meat in the stew she is purchasing, and the plate of the man behind her is filled with meat, she complains and storms out, infuriated by the argument of the woman serving that men are always given more meat. As a child Sara knew that if one of her siblings had been a boy, he would have been allowed access to Smolinsky's holy books, a privilege denied to daughters. Courageously, Sara turns down a wealthy real estate speculator's marriage proposal because she can't stand his materialist values and because she would rather go to college than marry.

In Reb Smolinsky, Yezierska created a character of Dickensian proportions. Smolinsky is a powerful antagonist for Sara. He is an unredeemed patriarch: an egotistical, selfish, misogynistic, hypocrital, and learned fool. The portrait of this selfish father, hiding behind his religiosity in order to avoid working, is the most powerful male figure in all Yezierska's canon. The uprooted tyrant marries off three of his daughters to men they don't love in order to obtain money for himself from supposedly wealthy suitors. He makes three of them bitterly unhappy. From the day he married his 14-year-old bride, he has made her unhappy. However, in the end his is something of a pathetic figure as he must live with the one female in his life who has escaped his tyranny.

Rifkeh Smolinsky is the all-suffering, all accepting, fabled Jewish mother, who understands her husband's foolishness but is loyal to the end of her bitter days. Rifkeh can be charmed by a few lines in Hebrew from her husband's mouth even though she can't understand the words. All Reb Smolinsky has to do is recite a short passage from the Torah or Talmud, and her anger melts into adoration. Rifkeh unfortunately was married as a child to this much older man, who took over her late father's business and ruined it, thus forcing the Smolinskys to emigrate to America. This dominated mother is the opposite of her independent, free-thinking youngest daughter. They contrast two generations: Old World submissive women and their liberated American daughters.

Bessie, Mashah, and Fania, are distinctive and richly defined supporting characters whose lives are in themselves interesting but sad.

THEMES

Throughout the canon of her work, Yezierska reiterates her main theme: the transformation through great effort of young immigrant women from greenhorn status to that of educated, productive, modern Jewish Americans. In Yezierska's stories, the WASP (White Anglo-Saxon Protestant) male is adored as the most desirable of men, especially if he is an educator. He is almost god-like, an unreachable goal for the young female Jewish immigrant, who has serious crushes on unlikely choices such as the two teachers Sara falls for in *Bread Givers*. When Sara finally is mature enough and ready for a permanent relationship, she does accept a Jewish lover, the principal of the elementary school she teaches in. He, however, is fully Americanized to the point that he knows no Hebrew, but is willing to learn the sacred language from Reb Smolinsky.

The title *Bread Givers* is thematically ironic. In the Orthodox immigrant Jewish family the father, preoccupied with religion, is not the bread giver. The bread givers in the Smolinsky family are the daughters who slave for their father. He is the parasite, living off the wages of the three older daughters and permitting them to marry only men who have or seem to have money he can extort from them.

Another important theme is that of America as a land of opportunity with values different from those of Eastern Europe. In the America of the beginning of the twentieth century, a woman was able to earn her own living, live on her own, receive a full education, fight her way out of poverty, become a professional person, and marry for love—impossibilities in the patriarchal shtetls of Russia and Poland.

NARRATIVE STYLE

In *Bread Givers* Yezierska created a parade of exotic (to the general reading public) characters speaking in the fractured Yiddish-inflected English of the ghetto, a language she made to sound almost poetic. The novel's first-person dialogue sounds like a translation from Yiddish, and it maintains the broad humor, subtle ironies, and word order of that eloquent and trenchant language that derived from Medieval German.

The novel is episodic. Each section could be a short story, and the episodes proceed chronologically as Sara matures from 10 years old, when she is a precocious child searching for pieces of coal in dust bins to warm her family, to the age of 27, when she is a successful elementary school teacher.

Bread Givers is structured by the fates of the four sisters, the father, and the mother. The early chapters depict the heart-breaking disasters of the marriages of Bessie, Mashah, and Fania. In the middle of the story Reb Smolinsky's business fiasco is exposed, and the final section of *Bread Givers* depicts Sara's education, her return to her family as her mother lay dying, her professional success, the finding of a romantic partner, and her reconciliation with, and new respect for, Reb Smolinsky.

HISTORICAL CONTEXT

Bread Givers depicts the severe hardships faced by Jewish immigrants in the high immigration period from 1881 to 1924. Furthermore, it focuses on the role of women in a patriarchal society, and, through Sara's story, it shows the strength needed to break the grip of a selfish patriarch who has inflicted great suffering on the women in his family.

Married immigrant women often accompanied their husbands to America, as did Rifkeh Smolinsky, along with her daughters. Sometimes the wife and children remained in Europe, while her husband earned enough money to bring his family to New York. This would be the only time the woman would not be subject to continuing pregnancies. When sent for by her husband, she became responsible for bringing the children to the emigration ports and keeping them safe during the long and difficult voyage to America.

On the Lower East Side the mother's duties were exhausting. Besides taking care of the children, sometimes bearing more, she cooked, did all the laundry by hand (a full day's work once a week), nursed the sick, fed the boarders, cleaned up after everyone, and often did piecework for local sweatshops.

Young single women like Sara, without English, generally found work as domestic servants, a much despised occupation. Young women working in factories soon made enough money so that they could exert some independence if they were strong enough, like Sara, to battle traditional familial and patriarchal values. They could hold back some of their earnings for stylish clothes and cosmetics in order to face what was a greater challenge than any job. They had to win a husband, preferably one with a good job and some savings. Unfortunately, societal pressures to marry and have children drove them back into the kind of domestic subservience they thought they had escaped. The profession of marriage broker was a lucrative one on the Lower East Side. Even an amateur blunderer like Reb Smolinsky found eager clients.

Sara's escape from a life of servitude to a father, a boss, or a husband was only possible in the United States because of educational and economic opportunities. Thus, coming to America for young, single female Eastern and Southern European immigrants was an act of liberation.

SUGGESTED READINGS

Primary Sources

Yezierska, Anzia. *All I Could Never Be*. New York: Persea, 1999.
———. *Bread Givers*. New York: Persea, 1999.
———. *Red Ribbon on a White Horse*. New York: Persea, 1987.

Secondary Sources

Henriksen, Louise Levitas. *Anzia Yezierska: A Writer's Life*. New Brunswick, N.J.: Rutgers University Press, 1988.
Schoen, Carol B. *Anzia Yezierska*. Boston: Twayne, 1982.

3

Michael Gold
Jews Without Money
(1930)

For most of his life, Michael Gold, who demonstrated his affinity with the working class by wearing baggy and often unwashed clothes over an unclean body, using rough language, and living a Spartan existence, preferred to be called plain, proletarian-sounding Mike Gold. Despite the passing of generations, Gold's Whitmanesque image lingers on. Today, he is more admired and appreciated than he ever was in his lifetime.

In none of Michael Gold's writings did he ever make clear the line between autobiography and fiction, and so it is best to call *Jews Without Money* a semi-fictional novel. It is based largely on his own childhood experiences, and it is one of the great documents on family life in New York City's Lower East Side ghetto at the beginning of the twentieth century. At the same time, *Jews Without Money* is a powerfully effective, vivid, antibourgeoisie depiction of the sufferings of the impoverished working class. The book employs course, brutal images and words of the mean streets, like kike, yid, nigger, and wop as it cries out for social justice for the poor in American society.

BIOGRAPHICAL CONTEXT

Michael Gold, the author of *Jews Without Money*, the most famous proletarian narrative that came out of the Great Depression, was born in 1893 as Itzok Isaac Granich on the Lower East Side of Manhattan. In elementary school his name was changed to Irving and then Irwin—each change less

Jewish sounding. In 1921 he adopted the pen name of Michael Gold, either because he admired an older radical with that name, or more likely because he tried to avoid being swept up in the U.S. government's raids on radical organizations and individuals following the Red Scare that marred the American political landscape immediately after World War I. The Russian Revolution of 1917 and the subsequent rise of international Communism polarized the American public in the 1920s and 1930s just as the early stages of the Cold War polarized us from the late 1940s through the 1960s.

Gold's parents, Chaim Granich and Gittel Schwartz Granich, came to the Lower East Side from Romania. Gold's father learned how to make men's suspenders, and, as a small manufacturer, he contracted to make one small part of suspenders' sets. Eventually, his storefront shop failed, and he had to go on the streets as a pushcart peddler in order to support a family of four. Gold never forgot his father's humiliation. He was never able to believe in the capitalist system again.

As was the custom for poor children at the time, Gold left school early. At the age of 12 he had a full-time job with the Adams Express Company as a night porter and later as a teamster when that meant driving a team of horses hitched to a delivery wagon. He also worked as an errand boy in the garment industry, a shipping clerk, and a printer's devil. In 1912 he began to study journalism at night at New York University. In 1914 he took classes at Harvard. That year, at a rally of unemployed men and women at Union Square in Lower Manhattan, Gold, a bystander at first, was roughed up in a brutal charge by police with truncheons. From that moment on, and until the end of his life, Gold was a radical.

In 1917 Gold began to write for the important radical periodical *The Masses*, where he was mentored by the radical intellectual Max Eastman. He joined the Communist Party after moving to Greenwich Village, where he poured out political poetry, articles, and stories. When the United States entered World War I in 1917 and instituted a military draft, Gold fled to Mexico to avoid it. There he labored on a ranch and in oil fields until the war was over and he could return to New York City. Gold edited *The Liberator* in 1921 and then moved to San Francisco.

Writing plays was Gold's main literary pursuit in the early 1920s. His friends in the avant-garde included the novelist Theodore Dreiser, and the playwrights Eugene O'Neill and Susan Gladspell. Eugene O'Neill's Province-town Players in Greenwich Village put on some of Gold's plays, but they had limited success. John Reed, the most famous American communist and the only American buried in the Kremlin, was another friend. Unlike many of his friends, Gold was never a radical theorist. He didn't work at understanding

Karl Marx. He merely embraced and endorsed popular Marxist views, which he presented in the most inflammatory way possible. Gold's lifelong commitment to radicalism was with the heart, not the mind.

In 1925 Gold went to the Soviet Union to study theater and write more radical plays. Returning to the Unites States without having been disillusioned by the terrible conditions in the Soviet Union, Gold founded the radical *New Playwrights Group*, which produced early plays by John Dos Passos and other writers on the Left.

Gold had been working on a fictionalized version of his childhood and youth for a dozen years. Finally, in 1930, the year the Great Depression fiercely gripped the country, *Jews Without Money* was published through the urging of the famous social critic H. L. Mencken. It was an immediate and outstanding success, going through 11 editions just in the first 12 months. After struggling as a writer for so many years, Gold was now hailed as the American equivalent of Maxim Gorki, the Russian literary master of stark naturalism. The book has not been out of print since the original publication. *Jews Without Money* had stirred the collective American conscience. The short-lived Proletarian Literature Movement—literature written for and by workers—had found its model and its masterpiece.

Lauded by many American writers such as Edmund Wilson and Sinclair Lewis, Gold was given the job of coeditor of the *New Masses*. Soon the old Lower East Side street fighter began long feuds in print with major American writers including Ernest Hemingway, Archibold MacLeish, Robinson Jeffers, Sherwood Anderson, and Thornton Wilder. In Gold's mind, conventionally liberal writers were sell-outs and tools of the capitalist exploiters.

In 1933 Gold began to write for the long-lived, and once widely circulated American Communist newspaper, *The Daily Worker*. In *The Hollow Men* (1941), Gold attacked writers who had abandoned Communism after the cynical Nazi-Soviet nonaggression and friendship pact of 1939. Despite the revelations of Stalinist terror and anti-Semitism, Gold remained loyal to Communism all his life. But after America entered World War II in 1941, Gold faded into obscurity. He started many literary projects and completed few.

In 1950, in the light of new anti-Communist witch-hunting in the American Congress and media, Gold moved to France with his wife and their two sons. He was poor once more. In 1957 he returned to the United States, settling in San Francisco for the remainder of his life. There he again wrote for the *Daily Worker* and also for *People's World*, for which he wrote a serialized sequel to *Jews Without Money* that was not well received. Today, students of American radicalism still study the 32 years of his *Worker* column: "Change the World." Gold died in 1967.

PLOT DEVELOPMENT

The hero of *Jews Without Money* is Mikey, an American-born Jewish boy living on Chrystie Street on the Lower East Side of Manhattan at the beginning of the twentieth century. He is a member of a gang of boys—Mikey, Nigger, Jake, Joey, Abie, Izzy, Harry, Stinker, and Pishteppel—who steal fruit from poor peddlers, use dead cats as missiles to be thrown at their enemies, taunt prostitutes, beat up strangers on their street, and enjoy their summers swimming in the filthy East River. The novel, a painful naturalist story of growing up in poverty, is in some ways a combination of Charles Dickens's *Oliver Twist* and Mark Twain's *Huckleberry Finn.*

Mikey's best friend is the contumacious Nigger (so named because of his dark complexion), a tough Jewish kid, who, driven by poverty and injustice, eventually becomes a gangster. Gold, by the way, spares no ethnic or racial group in realistically using the slurs and taunts of the violent slums: kike, yid, wop, mick, and others. Contumely is the standard exchange between ethnic groups. Gold's Lower East Side was neither melting pot nor mosaic, but a fierce ethnic and racial battleground. The city is the Wild West for the children of Eastern European Jewish immigrants. The Indians are the Irish and Italian gangs that must be fought off.

The vividly portrayed cast of characters in *Jews Without Money* includes pimps, boxers, drug fiends, pedophiles, corrupt and brutal Irish cops, prostitutes, rabbis, cruel Hebrew teachers, gangsters, unscrupulous politicians, sympathetic doctors, greedy doctors and landlords, arrogant social workers, Irish neighbors, and poor Jewish women and men.

Gold foregrounds sex in his portrait of the ghetto. It is widely for sale. Young male and female children are at risk from pedophiles. Women are used and abused. Gang rape and forced prostitution are common. Young boys are able to witness men fornicating with prostitutes. Women are also sexually harassed by factory owners and supervisors.

The backyard of Mikey's tenement was once a small cemetery, and the headstones now pave the yard. Symbolically, the boys dig up the graves of those early New York City settlers and cart off their bones for their collections. Gold is saying that New York belongs to the living young, who have no respect for, nor need of, the past.

Jews Without Money depicts Mikey's life from the age of 5 to 15. He lives in a wretched tenement flat with his mother, Katie, an immigrant from Hungary; his father, Herman, an immigrant from Romania; his younger sister, Esther; and an unnamed baby brother who arrives late in the story.

Mikey excels in school despite the fact that some of his teachers are bigots and the classes are overcrowded. However, he hates the Hebrew school he must attend in the afternoons, because the teacher is ignorant and foul-smelling and the lessons meaningless to Mikey because he is never taught the meanings of the Hebrew words he chants.

Running with his gang, the Chrystie Street Boys, he has adventures and misadventures, especially when he wanders out of his neighborhood and into such foreign territory as Little Italy.

Through Mikey's eyes we see the fall of his family. Mikey's father, Herman, is a house painter. But shortly after he came to America, he went into manufacturing with a cousin who cheated him out of the business. The cousin disappeared and Herman is obsessed with the betrayal. He is never able to go back into business, because he could never raise the $300 needed to start up again.

Herman regularly becomes ill from paint fumes. The lead-filled paint is ruining his lungs and stomach. Herman and Mikey are close. The father is proud of his bright son. He takes pleasure in telling Mikey about the adventures he had in coming to America. He hopes that Mikey will become a doctor, but in America Jews without money can't send their children to medical school.

When Herman's scaffold falls and his feet are smashed, he is unable to work for a year. When he tries to go back to work he can't face the scaffold, and as he has no other skill, he remains unemployed. Herman had bought into the American dream of prosperity and happiness for all. But one accident destroyed his hopes and his confidence, and he comes to understand that his son also could not possibly escape the grinding poverty of the ghetto on his own.

Katie, the strong, loving mother, becomes the breadwinner, working in a cafeteria while her husband is incapacitated. She can even take on the hated landlord when she and Herman don't have enough money for the rent. Mikey sells newspapers on the street to add to the family income. Then the worst tragedy that can happen to a family occurs: the death of a child.

Mikey's younger sister, Esther, with whom he often fights, takes over the housekeeping chores when Katie goes out to work in the cafeteria. One snowy winter evening, when she goes out of the flat to find wood for the stove, she is accidentally struck down by an express wagon. She falls between the horses, the heavy wheels run over her, and she dies in the hospital. The family is overwhelmed with grief. There seems no end to their troubles. Katie is devastated. All she can do is cling to Mikey and his little brother.

The depressed Herman becomes a pushcart peddler and is unable to feed the family on his meager earnings from selling bananas. At the age of 12 Mikey must forego high school and go to work in a factory where the work is brutal. One day he hears an East Side orator speak passionately of Socialism, and Mikey joins the workers' revolution.

Fortunately, *Jews Without Money* is not a vehicle for communist propaganda. The doctrinaire revolutionary cant is added on in only a dozen lines at the end of the text, when Gold elevates the workers' revolution to the status of a messianic religion.

CHARACTER DEVELOPMENT

Gold created his finest literary character, Mikey, as an American boy, a Huckleberry Finn under gaslight. And Nigger is his Jim, who teaches Mikey about respect, honor, and revenge, such as when he banged a racist schoolteacher on the nose when she called Mikey a little kike. Mikey and Nigger are the new American inner-city youth—tough, clever, street fighters on the make. Katie teaches Mikey about God, and he hopes for a Jewish Messiah who will look like Buffalo Bill and will smite the hateful gentiles. For Mikey the Messiah is as good as Santa Claus, maybe better.

Katie is drawn in the sentimental, venerating tradition of the self-sacrificing, all-loving, tough, pious, Jewish mother—a stereotypical characterization embraced as doctrinaire truth by Anzia Yezierska, Henry Roth, and many other Jewish American writers. This adoration, particularly in male Jewish writers, seems to be accompanied by a degree of authorial guilt, as if the classic Oedipal complex was universally a problem for Jewish men.

Katie is a cook, baker, cleaner, sage, and nurse. In a pinch she can midwife for a neighbor. Although she is disappointed with her husband and a chronic worrier, she loves her family to the extent that she would die for them; yet she scolds them continually. Katie is so compassionate that she is willing to go hungry herself rather than see other people starving. Having born the burden of seemingly caring for the world, she breaks when Esther is killed. The death of a child is the one blow from life she can't bear.

Herman is a caring father, if not a good provider. We see him through Mikey's adoring eyes: a fascinating storyteller and a good man, but also a dreamer, a foolish critic of collective interests and action, and a man betrayed by his belief in the American dream that prosperity is just around the corner. As Katie is broken by the loss of Esther, Herman is broken by the loss of his dream.

Katie's younger sister—Mikey's attractive Aunt Lena—is a true socialist woman. She goes on strike for better conditions and decent wages with her fellow workers. She walks a picket line all day and is beaten by strikebreakers and a cop. Lena is a young woman of principle. She has received a marriage proposal from a kind-hearted physician who could give her a better life than she has as a factory worker, but she turns him down because she is in love with a union leader on strike with her.

Next to Mikey, Nigger is the most interesting of the boys in the gang. He is wise, brave, and a natural leader. He has a sharp sense of justice and will fight for it. When a petty crook and pimp, Louie One-Eye, has offended him, he leads a posse of boys who slaughter Louie's prize pigeons. When life makes him a criminal, the first person Nigger kills is Louie who has made a prostitute of his sister.

Mikey's saintly kid sister, Esther, bears his bullying with grace and forgiveness. She envies his male freedom to roam with a gang or ride next to the hearse driver to and from the cemeteries in Brooklyn. Her violent death is a martyrdom to the brutalities of life in a ghetto.

THEMES

In *Jews Without Money*, Gold illustrates the destructive power of poverty. Slum life is life in a jungle. People are ground down by atrocious living conditions, lack of employment, unfair labor practices, and the general indifference of the wider society. Gold shows the effects of rampant, unregulated capitalism and patriarchal power on the working poor in such instances as when a rapacious landlord, who fully knows that prostitution is evil, prefers to rent apartments to prostitutes because he can charge them two to three times the amount he could charge a family. Gold believes that his America is rich and fat because, like a living colossus, it has fed on millions of immigrants.

Gold is against organized religion. Prayers have no efficacy. God surely did not conceive bed bugs and everything else that plagues humankind. Mikey can't understand why God let a friendly, poor old cart horse die in the streets. In *Jews Without Money*, believers are often hypocrites. Revered Hassidic Rabbis are treated like princes while exploiting and betraying their congregations.

Gold, like an anarchist, rails against the state that makes hardened criminals out of petty offenders. A boy who injured his father to stop him beating his mother is sent to a reformatory where he is savagely lashed with a belt until the buckle destroys one of his eyes. That boy returns to a society he hates and will become a hardened criminal. Most of all, Gold despises the nouveau riche, Jewish or gentile. Gold paints them savagely; they are disgustingly gross and excessively selfish.

Gold extols the all-sacrificing Jewish mother. She is the family bastion. She is a model of virtue. She rules the home, and she usually is victorious in her struggles with her husband. One mother described by Gold lives in a damp basement eating bread and drinking tea so her son can go to medical school.

He gets his degree, and she dies. The doctor wonders if it was worthwhile. Can one be proud in the grave?

An overriding theme in *Jews Without Money* is the need of workers to form unions in order to raise the standard of living for the entire community. The ultimate solution, as expressed on the last page of the novel, lies in Socialism, or the workers' revolution.

NARRATIVE STYLE

Jews Without Money is an aesthetically significant naturalistic narrative. Alone of all of Gold's writing—poems, plays, reams of journalism—it has achieved a permanent place in America literature. It depicts generation conflicts, cultural clashes, strife, and family tragedy that seem even now to hurt the inner-city poor more than any other social class.

Jews Without Money is a modernist work in that it employs an urban dialect in a way not unlike James Joyce's use of Dublin dialect in *Portrait of the Artist as a Young Man*. Gold's diction is a dense, brutal, muscular, and caustic oral language—an echo of the din, clatter, and roar of the teeming streets of the Lower East Side. Gold's style is journalistic. He uses short sentences like a boxer jabbing. The novel is rich in imagery, literal and figurative. It shouts rebellion in its disrespect for authority, decorum, and literary convention. Even today it is shocking. The plot is episodic and loosely structured. The narrative produces a dark, meandering, street carnival of grotesqueries, sex, and pain. It is neither sentimental about immigrant family life, nor for a childhood in the filth, cruelty, and brutality of ghetto life.

Gold's main audience for *Jews Without Money*, like Cahan's for *The Rise of David Levinsky*, is the general American reading public of his time. It is sensational, riveting, and unrelenting in its political messaging. A secondary audience is the English-reading immigrant population, eager to see images of themselves and their lives, harsh as they may be, presented to, and made a part of, the American scene in the first half of the twentieth century.

Gold set out to "photograph" the ghetto of his childhood. Gold's Lower East Side is a clash of communities: the gangs of boys banding together for self-protection on the streets; the sisterhood of housewives and whores, Jewish and gentile, helping each other survive the oppression and exploitation of men; workers in factories battling bosses; and religious Old World Jews struggling unsuccessfully to maintain obsolete values and a fast-eroding culture.

HISTORICAL CONTEXT

This incendiary, propagandistic novel documents the perceived need of Jewish workers for socialist organizations and unions. The Jewish labor movement began about the time of Gold's birth. On May Day 1890 thousands of Jewish workers marched out of the Lower East Side to Union Square (Fourteenth Street) demanding an eight-hour day. Jewish unions also focused on cooperative housing, insurance plans, and educational activities. This direction was the result of compassionate teachings in the Talmud and the reading of Karl Marx by Russian Jewish immigrants like Cahan who were well educated in Europe.

Naturally, the Jewish unions supported the once powerful Socialist Party. Gold uses Mikey's Dickensian experiences as a youth in the labor force to underline the need for restraint and reform of abuse by large corporations and small businesses. Fortunately, the early decades of the twentieth century were those in which the U.S. Congress began to enact antitrust legislation.

Samuel Gompers, an immigrant Jewish cigar maker, had founded the Federation of Organized Trades Unions of the United States and Canada in 1881. Five years later the name was changed to the American Federation of Labor (AFL). The New York City labor movement gained power because of the horrible Triangle Shirtwaist Company factory fire in 1911, when 146 workers burned or jumped to death. The fire escape door had been locked to prevent workers from leaving without permission. Most of the dead were young Jewish and Italian women. No one was convicted of any crime. The city was shocked. A young union leader, David Dubinsky, and a fledgling union, the International Ladies Garment Workers Union, led the protests. The result was that the New York State legislature passed a series of laws governing working conditions and workplace safety that were models for the national government.

SUGGESTED READINGS

Primary Source

Gold, Michael. *Jews Without Money*. New York: Carroll and Graf, 1984.

Secondary Sources

Angoff, Charles. *The Tone of the Twenties and Other Essays*. South Brunswick, N.J.: A.S. Barnes, 1966.
Folsom, Michael, ed. *Mike Gold: A Literary Anthology*. New York: International, 1972.

4

Henry Roth
Call It Sleep
(1934)

Call It Sleep, a modernist, stream-of-consciousness novel, is America's answer to Joyce's *Portrait of the Artist as a Young Man*. First published in 1934, *Call It Sleep* is the most significant masterpiece of the early Jewish American novel. This semi-autobiographical novel of a child's life on the Lower East Side at the beginning of the twentieth century is one of the most truthful and poignant depictions of the terrors of childhood ever written. Although Roth wrote a few short stories and, after an amazingly long hiatus, a tetralogy of novels under the group title of *Mercy of a Rude Stream* (1994–1998; last two volumes published posthumously), it is on *Call It Sleep* that his literary reputation rests.

BIOGRAPHICAL CONTEXT

Henry Roth was born in 1906 in Tysmienica, in what was then the Polish province of Galicia in the Austro-Hungarian Empire and now is a town in Ukraine. His parents and grandparents were Orthodox Jews. Shortly after Roth's birth, his father, Herman Roth, a waiter, left him and his mother, Leah Farb Roth, while he emigrated to New York City to find work and prepare a new home for his family. When Henry was about 18 months old, his mother carried him across the Atlantic to Ellis Island where his father met his tiny family and brought them to a tenement flat in the Brownsville section of Brooklyn. The Roths lived in Brooklyn only briefly. In 1910 they moved to a tenement on East Ninth Street on the Lower East Side of Manhattan. Roth's sister Rose was born there. *Call It Sleep* is primarily based on the childhood years Roth spent on the Lower East Side.

In 1914 the Roths moved again, this time to East 119th Street in the Jewish section of Harlem in order to live near relatives. The eight-year-old, now in a community that had many Irish and Italians, continued the education he received on the Lower East Side. The security he felt in the more homogeneous Lower East Side gave way to insecurity when he was in close contact with anti-Semitic gentiles and their children. One result of the move was the weakening of the boy's faith in the religion of his parents, a partial cause of Roth's later atheism.

Roth's parents quarreled a lot. Herman was a bully to his wife and children. As a child Roth disliked his father immensely and loved his mother inordinately. His father came to symbolize brutality, violence, and terror in the child's world, and his mother represented beauty, grace, kindness, comfort, and shelter.

After elementary school the bright youth studied at Stuyvesant High School and De Witt Clinton High School, entering City College of New York in 1924. He published his first short story, "Impressions of a Plumber," in the City College literary magazine, *Lavender*. In 1927 Roth met the person who would coach him into serious authorship: Eda Lou Walton, a poet from New Mexico who was teaching literature at New York University in Greenwich Village. She was 12 years older than Roth; nevertheless, they became lovers, and she introduced him to the Greenwich Village radicals, writers, artists, and theater people who were the American literary avant-garde of the time.

When, in 1928, Roth moved in with Walton in her Greenwich Village residence on Morton Street, he was close enough to walk to the Lower East Side streets of his formative childhood years. Shortly afterwards, he began to write about those agonized and traumatic years, primarily because he did not want to forget them. Surely Michael Gold's recently published semi-autobiographical novel *Jews Without Money* was on his mind.

Roth and Walton lived together for 10 years. She supported him financially and emotionally as he wrote. She was his substitute mother. Through Walton, Roth met such literary luminaries as Hart Crane, Mark Van Doren, and Louise Bogan. In 1930 Roth accompanied Walton to her residency at the Yaddo writers' colony in upstate New York, where he remained outside in a hotel, writing, while she worked and fraternized with other creative residents. Walton believed in Roth's talent. She gave Roth confidence as a writer, introduced him to modernist writing through T. S. Eliot's "The Wasteland" and

James Joyce's *Portrait of the Artist as a Young Man* and *Ulysses*, and encouraged his efforts on *Call It Sleep*. Initially, Roth began to write an autobiography, but he quickly changed to a modernist novel, part expressionistic and part naturalistic. In 1934, after four years of work, the book was published by Robert Ballou with the subsidization of Walton's friend David Mandel. Roth dedicated the novel to Eda Lou Walton.

Roth professed to be a Marxist, so he joined the Communist Party in 1933. He never intended to write a proletarian novel, nor imitate Gold's inflammatory *Jews without Money*, but the radical press expected a revolution-inspired text, and they were perplexed and angered by *Call It Sleep*. Other critics did not as yet understand the intricacies of a psychological stream-of-conscious novel. All of these reactions upset Roth.

However, some less biased and more perceptive critics recognized the book's original and powerful employment of language and its structural strength. All in all, however, the novel made only a slight impression on the literary scene. The fact that *Call It Sleep* came out in the height of the Depression, and that the publisher went bankrupt soon after publication, did not help either. Yet it did impress the leading book editor of the time, Scribners' Maxwell Perkins, who, in 1936, gave Roth an advance on a second novel. Roth started a work about an injured factory worker who becomes a communist and labor organizer. Unfortunately, while doing research one day on the New York waterfront, Roth was attacked and beaten by a pack of union thugs. Discouraged, he abandoned the nearly completed novel.

Roth then tried to start a narrative based on his adolescence, but his inability to write a proletarian novel that matched his political convictions seemed to have caused a near total writer's block for many years—indeed there was a hiatus of 50 years between novels that came to an end in a veritable tsunami of words, the four volumes of *Mercy of a Rude Stream* (1994–1998), which in fact are based on Roth's adolescence. But in the meantime, *Call It Sleep* had long faded from the public's collective memory and awaited rebirth.

In 1939, a year after separating from Walton, Roth married Muriel Parker, a composer. From 1939 to 1941 Roth, while writing a few short stories, taught night school English at Theodore Roosevelt High School in the Bronx. The *New Yorker* published "Broker" and "Somebody Always Grabs the Purple" in 1939. That year Roth became disillusioned with the Communist Party in America because, in mindless lockstep with international Communism, it supported the Nazi Germany-Soviet Union Friendship and Non-Aggression Treaty. However, Roth did not formally leave the party until 1956.

During World War II Roth performed war work as a precision tool grinder in New York City, Boston, and Providence. Henry and Muriel's two sons, Jeremy and Hugh, were born during the war. After the war, the Roths decided to leave hectic urban life and move to a rural locale. They chose a place very far from the madding crowds of New York City: outside of Montville, Maine.

Roth did what he could to support his family. He taught in a one-room schoolhouse and fought fires for the Forestry Service. In 1949 the Roths bought a small farm near Augusta, Maine, and Henry found employment as an attendant in Maine State Hospital until 1949 when he and Muriel tried to earn a livelihood raising ducks and geese. Roth also tutored pupils in various high school subjects. Muriel took up teaching as well and eventually became an elementary school principal.

Roth basically quit writing in Maine, but the *New Yorker* published one story in 1956, and *Commentary* brought out two autobiographical pieces in 1959 and 1960. Then, a literary miracle happened. Previously, in 1956 editors of *American Scholar* asked various literary critics, scholars, and historians to indicate their choice of the most undeservedly neglected book of the past 25 years. Two leading Jewish intellectuals, Leslie Fiedler and Alfred Kazin, picked *Call It Sleep*. So in 1960 Pageant Books reissued Roth's novel. It stirred up an unexpected amount of interest. Consequently, a mass market publisher, Avon Press, brought out a paperback version and, thanks to a rave review in the *New York Times Book Review* of October 25, 1964, by Irving Howe, another Jewish critic and intellectual, *Call It Sleep* became an international best seller. Roth was now elevated to the status of a major twentieth-century American writer.

In 1965 Roth was awarded a grant from the National Institute of Arts and Letters, with which he traveled to Mexico and Spain. In 1967 Roth finally and fully ended his sympathy for Communism when the Soviet Union supported the Arabs during Israel's fight for survival in the Six-Day Arab-Israeli War. Feeling that he had had a Jewish rebirth, in the late 1960s and 1970s Roth visited Israel contemplating emigration, but he decided against it because he was not familiar enough with the language and culture.

In 1968, upon Roth's receipt of a D. H. Lawrence Fellowship at the University of New Mexico, and after Muriel Roth retired from teaching in Maine, the Roths moved to Albuquerque, New Mexico. Roth had enjoyed and been inspired by a stay as a writer-in-residence at the D. H. Lawrence ranch in Taos. He began to work on *Mercy of a Rude Stream*, his massive series of novels based on his life after his childhood on the Lower East Side.

In 1987 *Shifting Landscapes*, a collection of Roth's short stories, articles, and interviews, was published. Muriel died in 1990, and Roth continued to work on *Mercy of a Rude Stream* until his death in 1995.

PLOT DEVELOPMENT

Call It Sleep is the story of the childhood of David Schearl, an immigrant boy. It begins in the "Prologue," when he is two years old. Then we observe his tormented life from six through eight in the main text. David, the Biblical name that translates from Hebrew as "beloved," is an extremely sensitive, Oedipal, Jewish boy, who, in the first years of the twentieth century, is removed at the age of two from his native land and thrust into the terrifying worlds of working-class Brownsville and the Lower East Side. Schearl translates from the Yiddish as scissors. The name implies that David's father, the jealous Albert Schearl, is trying, psychologically of course, to castrate his rival, David. But the name Schearl is David's too, and in him it symbolizes his need to cut himself off from the power of his father and, perhaps, the smother love of Genya in order to achieve selfhood. Lastly, David will cut himself off from his religion.

Structurally, the novel consists of the "Prologue" and four parts: "The Cellar," "The Coal," "The Picture," and "The Rail."

In "Prologue" the year is 1907, and the reader joins onlookers observing the reunion of an immigrant family at the Ellis Island Immigration Center. Albert Schearl meets his wife, Genya, and only child, David, and is clearly displeased with them. His rude behavior produces a cold welcome. Something is clearly amiss in the relationship between wife and husband. Schearl takes it out on the hapless boy. Later it becomes clear that Albert suspects, wrongly, that David is not his biological child. It is true that before her marriage to Albert, Genya had an affair with a gentile who abandoned her, but David really is Albert's son. It is already obvious that David is to be tossed between his paranoid father's hatred and his mother's overprotective love.

In "The Cellar" David is approaching his sixth birthday. The cellar represents the id, the child's deep needs and fears, and the source for the beginning of the boy's emotional development. It is the first place outside of the nest-like apartment he must pass in order to reach the street. The door of the cellar bulges out as if something monstrous is trying to escape and grab him. The cellar, whose contents are unknown, terrifies David. It seems to bar his way to the freedom of the street. However, it must be encountered and dealt with daily.

In "The Cellar," David comes to sense that his father's false friend Luter is a threat to his relationship with his mother and to the fragile stability of his family. His subconscious mind senses the power and the dangers of sex. When he finds himself looking at his mother's cleavage the way Luter did, he purges himself of the thought of the pleasure and comfort that lies in the dark place between Genya's breasts.

David's friend Yussie Mink shows him a rat trap and describes in detail how it works. When the disgusted David learns that the rats come from the cellar, he is doubly terrified of the place. Yussie's sister Annie takes David into a closet to play "bad," and after explaining in gross terms how babies are made, she puts his hand on her genitals and offers to touch his. David is not ready for this, and he resists. It seems that all the dangerous places are areas of dark confinement. The sight of a black coffin with a dead man inside racks him with fear. His mother's gentle explanation of death slightly assuages that archetypal fear, but David is left with the vision of yet another cold, dark place in his future, the eternal grave.

Distraught because he sees Luter enter his house when his father is away, and convinced that Luter and Genya are playing the horrid sex game that Annie taught him, David wanders the streets until it is time to go home, only to find himself lost. Kind people try to help him, but they can't understand his pronunciation of the name of the street he lives on. At a police station the compassionate cops also try to determine where he lives. Finally Genya is found, and she brings the exhausted and terrified child home again, clutching a cake the cops have given him. Paradoxically, almost all the adult men David encounters are kinder to him than his own father.

Luter does not return to have meals with the Schearls, but instead acts guilty at the workplace he shares with Albert, who now cannot understand why his "friend" won't look him in the eye and avoids talking to him. The paranoid Albert, finding his one friendship sour, wants to beat Luter, but instead he accidentally catches his finger in a printing press, and wounded, he vows never to work as a printer again.

Genya is shaken by guilt over Luter's visit and her belief that she has caused the split that resulted in her husband's injury. She also worries that David may know that Luter visited her in the afternoon and could tell Albert, so she is both relieved and saddened that Luter is no longer in their lives.

In "The Picture," the Schearl family has moved from the sedate Brownsville section of Brooklyn to East Ninth Street and Avenue D on the vibrant, teeming Lower East Side. Life is harder there. In their tenement the Schearls must share a toilet with other families. Albert no longer has a day job. As a milkman he must leave for work at night and return early in the morning.

Despite Albert's displeasure, Genya's younger sister Bertha arrives from Europe to live with the Schearls. Aunt Bertha is gross, foul-mouthed, and ugly, but she is also tough and quite capable of taking Albert on. She is funny too. One of the few amusing scenes in the novel takes place when Bertha and David stumble onto the Metropolitan Museum of Art. They get lost in it and don't have the language ability to locate an exit. Finally, they shadow a couple until the unsuspecting pair decides to leave the museum, thus leading the exhausted aunt and nephew to an exit.

Eventually, Bertha finds a suitor, Nathan, a garment industry worker and a widower with two preteen daughters. When Nathan comes to dinner, vindictive Albert tries to destroy the relationship, but to no avail, for Bertha will marry her mousey suitor. They plan to buy a candy store and live in the back rooms with the two girls.

The central event of "The Picture" occurs when Genya buys a painting from a pushcart. It is a landscape of a field of corn and blue flowers. It reminds her of her homeland in Europe, and it helps her to sustain the memory of her happy moments in the fields with the gentile lover who abandoned her. Poor Genya's life with Albert is so miserable that except for loving David the only pleasure she has is looking at her picture.

Bertha pries Genya's secret from her: that she had a gentile lover, a handsome church organist named Ludwig. He was engaged to someone else, a rich gentile woman with a large dowry. Genya's parents found out about the relationship, and her father beat her. Six months later she met Albert, to whom she never revealed her first love. She is pushed into marriage with Albert by her parents. Unfortunately for Genya, David overhears the confession and understands more than his mother realizes. The picture and her son will betray her.

"The Coal" finds David, age seven, sent to a cheder, an afternoon Hebrew school, a Dickensian place run by a mean and filthy rabbi and attended by wretched boys who do not want to be there. In the cheder David learns that the lips of the prophet Isaiah were touched by a burning coal in the hands of an angel who got the coal from God's cellar. That is how Isaiah was able to speak to God. David associates the ability to speak to God with torment followed by salvation. Later in the novel David will learn that there is coal in the cellar, and envisioning the coal helps to bring him back to life after he has nearly electrocuted himself.

David proves to be an outstanding pupil in his Hebrew class, but he is unable to ask the rabbi about God. It is Genya who explains that God is power. When three Irish boys jump David, he denies his Jewishness. They show him the power of the electric trolley by making him drop a zinc sword in the channel of the charged rail. The sight of the blue electrical flash transfixes the child, and he thinks of Isaiah and the burning coal. Unwittingly, David has found the source of power that will redeem him at the end of the narrative. He even goes so far as to break into the locked cheder to find the book with the story of Isaiah in it. David is now a visionary as well as a traumatized child who will hurt many people and himself before he wins a truce from his father that resolves the Oedipal impasse, thus allowing him to have a more normal life. Meanwhile, Bertha has married and is now working hard in her own candy store and caring for her two wild, preteen step-daughters.

In "The Rail," the fourth and longest section of *Call It Sleep*, the Oedipal impasse continues as David, having been tormented by his father, and upset in the cheder, flees home to find his mother coming out of a bath in the washtub, wearing a damp, loose-fitting robe. The sight of secret parts of her body, and the feel of her flesh next to his, calms the overwrought child immediately. Shortly afterwards, on the street, his pals tell him how they peeped in a window and saw a naked woman in a washtub. It was Genya, and David is maddened to tears by the thought of this "violation" of *his* mother.

Meanwhile, Albert has bought a totemic picture for himself and hung it prominently in the front room of the flat. It shows a massive bull. It reminds him of the days he herded his father's cattle, and he let a bull gore his father to death. But the picture also symbolizes Albert's power over his wife, and even more deeply, as it has horns, it represents his continual suffering over the thought that he could have been betrayed by Genya back in Austrian Poland. Ironically, the only possible cuckolding came in America with his "friend" Luter. For David, the horns on the bull symbolize the threat to his life he knows he must face and answer in the future.

On the roof David sees a boy with a kite on another roof. He has blond hair and blue eyes. David knows that those features don't belong on East Ninth Street, a Jewish street. David wants to make friends with the stranger. Like his father, David needs a male friend, and like his mother, David is attracted to the different good looks of a gentile. Leo is a 12-year-old Polish American, and a lucky lad as far as David is concerned, because he has roller skates and no father. Leo points out a cross on a building and informs David that the Savior died on a cross. David is fascinated by the word "Savior." He needs a savior to save him from his father. Leo also is wearing a scapular with the Virgin and Child painted on it. He tells David that wearing it makes him unafraid. As David is afraid most of the time, he would like not to have fear. He can also relate to a picture of Mary adoring her child.

David is intrigued by the implied power of a rosary he sees in Leo's apartment, and is willing to bring his friend to his aunt's step-daughters in exchange for a broken one. Leo wants to have sex with the girls. David is so enamored of his older friend, who is so sure of himself, that David will even pimp for Leo. David receives the promised rosary just before Leo forces sex on 12-year-old Esther, but he also receives a beating from the outraged Esther and the revelation that his "friend" Leo is really another Jew-hater.

Frightened by the encounter with sex and religious hatred, David rushes to the cheder where he lies to the rabbi, Reb Yidel, to cover his distraught state by saying that his mother is dead, that she died long ago, and that the woman who first brought him to the rabbi was really his aunt. He further informs the rabbi that Aunt Bertha, his "other" aunt, had just revealed this "truth" to him. Using the fragment of information he learned from eavesdropping on Genya and Bertha, David builds on the lie by telling Reb Yidel that his "real" father was an organist in a church. This, of course, is the kind of information, possibly confirming his fear that David is illegitimate, that would drive Albert insane. David's "confession" is a manifestation of the boy's inward desire to have a different father, to be a Christian like Leo, to be a part of the safer and stronger majority, to have freedom and power, and, lastly, to be able to drop the seemingly unbearable burden of his parents' religion. Now all this is possible because he has a rosary.

Reb Yidel is perplexed. Suddenly, for six pages of text, the point of view shifts from David to the rabbi. Reb Yidel does not know what to do with David's revelations. After deliberation he goes to the Schearl residence to be met by Genya at the door.

Simultaneously, Esther's sister Polly informs her parents of what has happened to Esther. The pregnant Bertha and her husband, Nathan, fight over who was responsible for minding the children. Nathan runs out of the store to inform on David, whom he blames for the assault on Esther. Bertha follows to stop him before Albert finds out and beats David, but it is too late. David faces his parents and the rabbi when he arrives home after wandering the streets, fearing what is awaiting him. When the rabbi reports David's statements, a furious round of revelations and confessions ensues. Genya is terrified because Albert now knows what he suspected, that she had a lover before they were married. She was not a virgin bride. She was foisted off on him. Albert also incorrectly thinks that Genya was pregnant when they were married, and her parents purposely "lost" David's birth certificate which would indicate an earlier birth than was reported to him.

Genya now lets on that she had heard that Albert allowed his father to be gored to death by a bull, but she never believed the story. Albert demands to know who was David's father. Convinced that Albert is insane, Genya prepares to grab David and leave her husband immediately, when Bertha and Nathan break in. The scene is pandemonium. Bertha tries to prevent her husband from informing on David, but before Albert can beat the story out of Nathan, David starts to confess and hands his father his horsewhip to punish him. Now Albert is sure that David has done something terrible. When the child reveals all, Albert denies paternity and begins to whip David furiously. The rosary and a cross fall to the floor, further "evidence" to the shocked and amazed group that David is the son of a gentile. Albert is jumped on and held back from murder by Bertha and Nathan as Genya flings open the door and orders David to run for his life.

David dashes wildly, hysterically, through the streets. Coming upon a milk can, he takes the milk dipper and runs on to the trolley tracks where he intends to use the dipper as a wand to release the flaming blue power that could save him.

In order to extend suspense Roth briefly shifts the novel's point of view from David to a narration of the Avenue D environment through which a streetcar line cuts. The sounds of many accents pierce the air of the East Side Babel. Suddenly, people run to the area where a long burst of flame erupted, and they find that a child has been electrocuted. David has thrust the handle of the dipper into the crack in the power rail. It is a desperate, defiant, phallic act of thrusting and penetration to capture or to kill at the font of regenerative force.

With brooms the people sweep the body away from the charged rail as if it were refuse. The dipper is nearly destroyed. A doubtful policeman tries resuscitation. An ambulance jangles onto the scene and a medical intern jumps out. Applying artificial respiration, he discovers that David is not dead but struggling for his life.

As the point of view shifts back to David, the reader learns that inside his mind the child has found the burning coal of Isaiah shining as bright as a pearl. He, a first-born son, like Isaac in the Bible, has been snatched from the jaws of death. The resurrected child is borne to his home. His ankle has a second-degree burn, but otherwise, miraculously, David is unharmed. The family is shocked to see him carried in by a policeman, followed by the young doctor and a crowd. David feels triumphant as his father's face turns white with fear. Genya is screaming in anguish. People are pointing at Albert accusingly and speaking of a deadly quarrel. Questioned, Albert admits that David is his eight-year-old son. It is the triumphant moment for David. His father has acknowledged paternity.

In David's near self-sacrifice and willingness to serve as his mother's penance by immolating himself, the family crisis has passed. The thought of the near death of an only child overwhelms the suspicion, guilt, fear, hatred, and paranoia that have made the Schearl family so dysfunctional. Albert slinks off to buy medicinal oil, and David is comforted by Genya and urged to sleep. David can only call it sleep, for his mind remains active. He feels neither pain nor terror now. The Oedipal child senses that somehow he has won.

CHARACTER DEVELOPMENT

David Schearl, so unable to cope with all his problems and fears, needs tranquility. He searches for a power to bring him peace. David is a mystic.

He is in search of a faith, a redeemer, although, as a child, he cannot understand any of the driving motivations of his young life. David is engaged in the archetypal quest for salvation. He has his epiphany when he encounters the raw power of the rail. The crowd that comes to the aid of the stricken child thinks he is dead, but he comes back to life. The shock that racks his body energizes David and leaves enough stored power in his little body to give him the drive to endure the trials of his future.

David is revolted by the thought of sex. He was traumatized by his experience in the closet with Annie, and when he knows that his mentor Leo has forced sex with his cousin Esther in Aunt Bertha's cellar, he is again disgusted. The dank, dark cellar symbolizes the vagina, what Annie had called the "knish" into which men put their "pretzel." The thought that his mother could have had sex with Albert's "friend" Luter is unbearable to David, for his mother must be like the Christ child's mother, a virgin devoted only to him. In Freudian terms the cellar is the id. It is locked in a titanic struggle with the superego, the imposed, controlling, terrifying will of the father.

David achieves redemption at the novel's end. He has boldly liberated himself from Albert's tyranny, when the latter, himself shocked by David's near fatal execution, realizes how insanely he has acted toward his son. David has achieved the strength of individuality. He has repealed the primal law of the father.

It must also be said of David that although he is very sensitive and intelligent, he is not a likable child. David is a compulsive and skillful liar. Sometimes he seems malevolent in his unerring ability to reveal things that hurt people who care for him, and he is so attached to his mother that the reader now and then feels more sympathy for Albert than for David in their archetypal father-son struggle.

The portrait of Albert Schearl, who beats his six-year-old son with a clothes hanger and a horsewhip, and who wishes him dead, is a child's nightmare of a father. Because of Albert, David's wanderings in the dangerous labyrinthine Lower East Side must be seen as an unconscious attempt to escape torture or even death. Mother and son must huddle for mutual protection, while existing with the monster in the home. Like D. H. Lawrence's *Sons and Lovers*, another Freudian modernist story of a mother and son bonding against a father almost to the point of unnaturalness, *Call It Sleep* shows no mercy for the tormented and tormenting male parent.

In Europe, Albert, hating his father for his cruelty to him, let the older man die when he could have saved him. Clearly, Albert sees the father and son relationship as perpetually a confrontational one. As he betrayed his father, so he expects a betrayal from David. The way for the patriarch to save himself from the fate he doled out to his own father is to destroy his son.

Albert, who has trained to become a printer, an important trade, goes from job to job, because in his paranoia he sees slights and offenses everywhere. He is always seeking revenge for something. Eventually, no longer able to find work in the printing trade because of his reputation for anger and threatening violence, he becomes a milkman driving a horse and wagon on morning rounds, truly a comedown for a skilled craftsman. Albert is not only his son's enemy, he is his own enemy, too.

Genya Schearl is another fine characterization. Of course, she is one more saintly Jewish mother ready to do anything to protect her beloved son, but this Jewish mother is infused with warm sexuality and devoid of shrewishness. She has had a lover before Albert, whom she had to marry because she was, according to her parents, "damaged goods." Significantly, Genya, like Albert and David, was badly treated by her father. The three main characters in the novel suffered at the hands of the male parent.

The gentle and pretty Genya is courted and pursued by Albert's supposed friend Luter, who correctly surmises that this attractive woman was not having sex with her bullying husband. Genya's relationship with David is Oedipal to a fault, of course, but Roth is also offering her as a portrait of pure, instinctive, maternal love.

Like so many immigrant Jewish women who came to a country whose language is different from their native one, Genya exists in the prison of a small flat. Except for the shopping trips to the nearby pushcarts to buy food, she is never outside. When she must find her way to a police station to claim David after he has become lost, her journey is fearful for her. Ironically, her seven-year-old son has more mobility and travels farther in the neighborhoods than she ever does. During the entire course of the narrative, some six years including the "Preface," she has never learned English. Although her opportunities to learn are severely limited by the prescribed gender roles of wife and mother, she could have done more to acquire some fluency in the language of her adopted country. She is not saddled with roomers. She has only one child. The flat is tiny. But Genya is somewhat indolent and too content in the sphere of the home. She has made no friends even though there are dozens of Yiddish-speaking women around her. Her fear of her husband and his biting tongue may have prevented her from finding sisterly friends and inviting them into her home.

Roth's depiction of Aunt Bertha can only be described as gross. She is a mountain of flesh topped by a vulgar mouth. Her lust for dangerous information about her sister's earlier life and her inability to keep a sister's confidences cause much grief for the Schearl family. The reader senses a touch of misogyny in Roth's portrayal of the one strong woman in the narrative.

THEMES

A major theme in *Call It Sleep* is the problem of an ethnic minority trying to adjust to a new life, culture, and language in the overwhelming metropolis of New York. It is a problem experienced today by immigrants arriving daily from all over the world. The Schearls endure a double disinheriting, first from the Jewish village life in Europe into which they were born, and second when moving from the homogeneous Jewish community in Brownsville to the area of the Lower East Side called Alphabet City (because avenues have letter names: A, B, C, and D). This tenement area was inhabited by Irish, Italian, Polish, Hungarian, and Ukranian immigrants as well as Jews. Friction was constant. Living conditions were nearly intolerable. Roth's nightmarish vision of the ghetto environment is like a Dantean circle in hell.

As a Marxist, Roth attacks religion in *Call It Sleep*. Like Michael Gold he focuses on corrupt or inept rabbis, but he also attacks the prevalent anti-Semitism issuing forth from Roman Catholic teaching and preaching. Lastly, Roth, blames the material and cultural poverty of the urban poor on a capitalistic society.

Roth never mentions Sigmund Freud in the novel, but clearly *Call It Sleep* is informed by psychoanalytic theory. David is a case study of the Oedipus Complex: he loves his mother with a passion that borders on the erotic as he fantasizes about his mother's naked body. He is fiercely jealous of Luter's access to his mother. He is locked in a classical life and death struggle with his rival for Genya's love: Albert. His thrusting of the milk ladle into the dark gap in the rail and the resulting near parody of orgasm comes as he triumphs over his seemingly emasculated father, who slinks away to fetch medicine for him.

NARRATIVE STYLE

Roth employs a traditional plot in *Call It Sleep:* there is an expository prologue, reversals, strong conflicts, and satisfying closure with David's victory over his paternal Goliath. Almost the entire book is written from David's child's eye point of view. Roth strives successfully to have the reader totally experience David's inner and outer world. In stunning dialogue Roth displays a rainbow of dialects: Jewish American, Irish American, Italian American and mixed New York City street argot. He also portrays David's consciousness reacting to sacred and secular foreign languages that Roth expresses by converting foreign languages to their phonetic English equivalents.

The languages represented in the narrative include the Hebrew and Aramaic of the Hebrew Bible, and Polish, spoken when Genya reveals to Bertha that she had a love affair before marriage. Roth sees the Lower East Side as a place where languages and accents led to confusion, mistaken ideas, and dangerous assumptions. Language foils communication as much as it aids it. Lower East Side life flounders in cacaphonic confusion and linguistic anarchy, as if it were the Tower of Babel. Roth has David particularly dislike spending endless hours reading Hebrew Scripture in the cheder with little or no effort by the instructor to teach the meaning of the words.

Roth used correct English for the Yiddish speakers, reserving broken English for the occasions when his characters actually spoke in English. The English "translation" of Yiddish, as it comes from the mouth of the characters, is eloquent, while the broken dialect English is a crude street slang that purposefully grates on the ear. Roth is indicating his belief that there was a cultural loss when the Jewish immigrants slowly abandoned their native language for their new one. Nevertheless, Roth chose to write in English, his school language, not Yiddish, his mother tongue.

Significantly, David's English improves as he grows older. At first his Yiddish is good and his English is broken. Then halfway through the text, as he has grown older, his Yiddish and English are about equal. Empathizing with David, the reader experiences, serially, the pristine Yiddish his mother speaks (presented in perfect English), the authentically crude and obscene patois of the street, and the vivid, image-laden, monologue of the child's exploration of the landscape of self.

HISTORICAL CONTEXT

From the perspective of the beginning of the Great Depression and the early 1930s, Henry Roth created a panorama of ghetto life on the Jewish East Side of Manhattan in the first decade of the twentieth century. That decade in American history was the high point of Jewish immigration from Eastern Europe. A half million Jewish men, women, and children, most in families, poured into the city through Ellis Island, the scene of the "Prologue" of *Call It Sleep*. Some immigrants came to escape anti-Semitism, others came for economic opportunity, and a few, like Albert and Genya Schearl, came to escape dark elements in their past.

New York City spent vast sums of money to educate immigrant children in new schools. Settlement houses, like the Henry Street Settlement, the University Settlement, and the Educational Alliance, provided nursing services, English-language education, health information, and cultural activities to ease the entry into American civilization. The "Melting Pot" theory of assimilation into the greater society was current and effective. Yiddish language newspapers like the *Daily Forward* advised immigrants, helped reunite separated family members, and aided in finding employment. Jewish organizations like Mount Sinai Hospital, the Hebrew Orphan Society, the Hebrew Sheltering and Guardian Society, and the Hebrew Emigrant Aid Society stove mightily to ease the burdens of physical, cultural, and psychological transition from a world largely of small towns and villages, to urban life in the most populous city in the United States.

However, in Roth's depiction of immigrant life, these government and private institutions are invisible. The novel's perspective—a child's eye view—has the Schearl family struggling unaided against the harsh realities of the life of the working poor in early twentieth-century urban America.

SUGGESTED READINGS

Primary Source

Roth, Henry. *Call It Sleep*. New York: Farrar, Straus and Giroux, 1991.

Secondary Sources

Kellman, Steven G. *Redemption: The Life of Henry Roth*. New York: W. W. Norton, 2005.

Wirth-Nester, Hanna, ed. *New Essays on Call It Sleep*. Cambridge: Cambridge University Press, 1996.

5

Meyer Levin
The Old Bunch
(1937)

The Old Bunch is a story that follows a group of young Jewish men and women coming out of the slums of Chicago from high school in 1921 to 1934, the time of Chicago's Century of Progress World's Fair. It recounts their relationships, family life, and careers as they strive to comprehend what it means to be Jewish and American. Like Michael Gold's *Jews Without Money* and John Steinbeck's *The Grapes of Wrath* (1939), *The Old Bunch* is a major Proletarian novel. It is often compared to James T. Farrell's *Studs Lonigan* trilogy (1932 to 1935), the bitter portrait of Irish Catholic life on Chicago's South Side. *The Old Bunch* is an ambitious work of American art, epic in scope and length.

The Old Bunch was criticized by some members of the American Jewish community because they felt it presented an unfavorable view of Jewish America. The criticism was ill-founded. The novel presents a singular community in transition, and it does so as a naturalistic work of art, showing the virtuous and the vicious, the honest and the dishonest, and the idealists and the cynics. Some characters are idealistic and some are materialistic, as with any American ethnic group.

BIOGRAPHICAL CONTEXT

A prolific writer, Meyer Levin—author of 15 novels, many works of nonfiction, plays, and screenplays—never achieved the fame and critical acclaim that some of his Midwest contemporaries did, such as Ernest Hemingway and F. Scott Fitzgerald. Only two of his novels achieved considerable popular and critical success: *The Old Bunch* and the documentary novel *Compulsion* (1956). Most of Levin's work centered on Judaism and Jewish American life. He was one of the first American authors to engage the Holocaust. He envisioned Jews as positive human beings working for a brighter future despite the lamentable past and painful present. He was an early supporter of the nascent State of Israel. Indeed, he visited the pioneer Jewish communes in Palestine in the 1920s, and he eventually had a home in Israel where he died in 1981.

Meyer Levin was born in the Jewish immigrant ghetto on Chicago's West Side in 1905 to Joseph Levin, a tailor, and Goldie Levin, immigrants from Eastern Europe. It was an area in transition as many Italian immigrants were moving in. Levin started to write in elementary school, and he even managed to set up his stories in type and print them at a local print shop. Levin continued writing in high school and at the University of Chicago, which he entered in 1921. A year before he graduated in 1924, Levin got a job on the *Chicago Daily News*, where he rose from reporter to feature writer and then columnist. His column was called "A Young Man's Fancy." In 1925 that "young man's fancy" drew him, along with thousands of young Americans including F. Scott Fitzgerald and Ernest Hemingway (also a Chicago reporter), to Paris, the artistic capital of the world.

In Paris, Levin studied painting under Fernand Léger, a distinguished Cubist, who encouraged Levin, but also indicated that he had much to learn. Levin, however, was impatient for success, so he returned to the United States to resume work as a journalist and write his first novel, *Reporter,* which was published in 1929. Unfortunately, the novel was quickly withdrawn under the threat of a lawsuit by a newspaperwoman who claimed that she had been portrayed in the book. His publishers did not want the expense of defending the suit, and they asked Levin to agree to the withdrawal. Levin really did not think all that much of his first long work of fiction, so he agreed.

But before the *Reporter* fiasco the restless Levin went overseas once more, this time to Palestine where many young Jews from Europe and America were settling on purchased land in socialist agricultural communes called Kibbutzim and beginning to build the Jewish homeland that would eventually be called the State of Israel. Levin worked on a Kibbutz near Haifa and continued to write, completing his second novel, *Frankie and Johnnie* (1930), a bleak unsuccessful tale. Levin's third novel, *Yehuda* (1931), established his reputation as a novelist. Based on his commune experience, it is the first novel in English set in Jewish Palestine. However, the onset of the Great Depression forced Levin to return to the States where he settled in New York City and attempted, unsuccessfully, to make a career as an actor.

A writing opportunity appeared with a new magazine just going into print called *Esquire*, and Levin got the job of movie reviewer. During his five-year stint Levin wrote the novel that is generally recognized as his masterpiece, *The Old Bunch*, published in 1937. It is a raucous, overly-written (964 pages), gripping account of 20 Jewish youths in Chicago as their lives are tossed on the currents of history from their adolescence in the ebullient 1920s to their battered adult experiences in the Depression's most grim period, the early 1930s. Meanwhile, Levin married Mabel Schamp Foy in 1935. They had one son and divorced in 1942.

Other early novels include *New Bridge* (1933) about an evicted family in the Depression, and *Citizens* (1940), the fictionalized story of the shooting of Chicago steel mill strikers in 1937. Before the latter was published Levin went to Spain in 1936 to cover the Spanish Civil war. Naturally, he favored the democratic Loyalist side because the ultimately successful rebels were fascists supported by Hitler and Mussolini.

Back in America, Levin got a job as a screenwriter in Hollywood, but when the United States entered World War II after the treacherous Japanese attack on Pearl Harbor on December 7, 1941, he went to Washington to write propaganda films for the Office of War Information. Sent to London, he became a war correspondent, and in 1945 he was present at the liberation of Buchenwald and other concentration camps. Like the rest of the world, Levin was stunned and profoundly disturbed by the horrors the Germans had inflicted on so many innocent Jewish and other people. He would never forget the scenes of gas chambers, crematoriums, and hills of starved bodies.

Next Levin quickly returned to Palestine to cover the struggle of Jewish partisan organizations against the British and Arabs to bring the desperate survivors of the concentration camps into the only place in the world where they were wanted by at least a part of the population. The novel *My Father's House* (1947) is about that troubled period. In 1948 Levin married Tereska Szwarc, daughter of an artist he had met in Paris, and they had a son. The autobiography *The Search* appeared in 1950.

In 1951 Levin was back in New York City, trying to re-establish himself in the City's literary world, but an intriguing possibility drew him back to Chicago, where in 1924, as a cub reporter, he had attended the sensational murder trial of Richard Loeb and Nathan Leopold, young men who had murdered 14-year-old Bobby Franks for the thrill of it. The great defense lawyer, Clarence Darrow, defended the young men and saved them from execution. After reviewing the case, Levin wrote his most successful novel—financially speaking—*Compulsion* (1956). In doing so, he created a new subgenre of fiction, the "documentary novel," also called the "nonfiction novel," two later examples of which are Truman Capote's *In Cold Blood* (1966) and Norman Mailer's *The Executioner's Song* (1979). Levin's adaptation of *Compulsion* for the stage had a long Broadway run, and the 1959 film was also successful.

Levin was the first writer to dramatize *The Diary of Anne Frank*, but his version was not produced, and he, an umbrageous person, became deeply involved in litigation over the matter. Two works documented his frustration and struggle: *The Fanatic* (1964) and *The Obsession* (1973), his second autobiography. Indeed, Levin believed that he did not receive the literary reputation he deserved because of a conspiracy of critics.

Levin spent much of the last part of his life in Israel. That new country inspired four late novels: *Eva* (1959), *The Settlers* (1962), *Gore and Igor* (1968), and *The Harvest* (1978), the sequel to *The Settlers*. Levin's last novel, *The Architect*, is one of his best (published posthumously in 1982). When Meyer Levin died in Jerusalem in 1981, he left behind a diverse body of work that not only reflected the fascinating life he had led, but also chronicled the development of Jewish American consciousness in the twentieth century. That made him one of the most significant Jewish American writers of his time.

PLOT DEVELOPMENT

The Old Bunch is the collective story of the evolving lives of 12 Jewish boys and 8 Jewish girls who, early in the twentieth century, lived in the same Chicago neighborhood and who went to school together. It is also the story of their old-world parents whose crudeness, anxieties, and religious values are despised by their children in their rush to assimilate. The young are ashamed of their parents until they become parents themselves, and they begin to look to their Jewish roots for some comfort and security as the Germans begin the genocide of European Jewry in the 1930s.

The novel's light flashes back and forth focusing on one and then another of the young people as time passes from early in the Jazz Age into the Great Depression. The youth in *The Old Bunch* represent a certain segment—children of immigrants—of a generation of American society as it was absorbing vast numbers of immigrants. The young people in the novel form a collective entity whose development and change structure the work. Their individual selves and families are part of a vast tapestry depicting a particular time and place: Chicago in the 1920s and early 1930s.

The attitudes and actions of the friends develop out of their relationships with each other and the impact of their urban environment. They become doctors, lawyers, teachers, and business people. One becomes an artist who battles a society dominated by philistines. One is a gifted, but hard luck inventor, who naively loses the patent to a garage door opener that could have made him rich. One becomes a professional athlete who succeeds in his sport, bicycle-racing, and fails miserably as a businessperson. All the young men and women are upwardly mobile, trying to find a place in the greater American society. None of the young men become rabbis or Talmudic scholars, although one troubled soul, a cynical agnostic, tries studying for the rabbinate because he thinks it will lead to wealth and ease, but a marriage to a sympathetic gentile woman ends his hypocrisy. In Europe, rabbinical and Talmudic studies had the highest prestige among the Jewish population. In materialistic mid-America, assimilation devalued those endeavors.

An important plot line in *The Old Bunch* is the slow fall of the wealthiest parent of the members of the group, the high-living Rube Moscowitz, a scrap-dealing businessman, politician, and ward boss who has made his fortune by cooperating with Chicago's notoriously corrupt officials. Moscowitz and his family are initially seen as living an assimilationist high life, but like the fall of Rube's mentor Samuel Insul, an English-born utilities magnate whose financial collapse ruins hundreds of small investors, Moscowitz's fall is symbolic of the capitalistic dynamic: a slow and steady rise on the roller coaster of greed and dishonesty to heights of economic power, followed by a quick and catastrophic fall. A lawyer in the group—one of three—Sam Eisen, develops his skills as an orator and he devotes his life to defending the poor and the politically persecuted.

The City of Chicago in the early twentieth century looms like a mega-monster in *The Old Bunch*. Levin portrays it with Hogarth-like satire: an almost inconceivably corrupt metropolis. At one point, when the Chicago World's Fair is opening, the medical establishment hides the fact that amoebic dysentery is spreading from an abominably filthy hotel kitchen and endangering the lives of visitors to the city and residents alike. Nothing must discourage visitors from coming to Chicago for the fair and spending their money. Almost everyone in the story is a racist. Even some of the Jews, beset as they are with rampant anti-Semitism, use the n-word frequently and even call other Jews "kikes."

Runt Plotkin, one of the young men, claws his way up by being a part of the Chicago underworld. He starts as a crooked peddler who is always on the prowl for women. He goes to a third-rate law school and becomes a third-rate lawyer who specializes in defending mobsters. Ironically, he is brought down by an angry judge who wrongly punishes him for defending criminals. Another group member, Lou Margolis, also becomes a lawyer, and he connects to Moscowitz money by marrying Rube's daughter and embracing his political cynicism.

Some of the men in the group eventually take over their father's businesses, when the parent dies or is ruined in the Depression. Typically, Mort Abrahamson turns from a compassionate employer to a rabid capitalist who despises his workers. His venomous diatribes turn away his more rational, liberal acquaintances.

Almost incestuously, the women of the group marry the men of the group, have their children, try to direct their husbands toward more financially lucrative careers, and sometimes destroy their marriages through their materialism and need for control. The women strive to be either homemakers or schoolteachers.

Everyone in the old bunch is hurt by the Depression and some by anti-Semitism. A struggling doctor casts his lot with a medical cooperative and is punished by the medical establishment. A professional athlete who has invested in his father's business loses his money and returns to his sport. The other businessmen become brutally hard on their workers, especially if they have unionized to survive in those hard times.

The Old Bunch ends brilliantly, as Levin bundles all the story lives together in a series of newsreel-like, juxtaposed scenes during the 1932–1933 Chicago World's Fair. The novel's departing images are of the glittering fair. It is a superficial, ephemeral, fast-decaying mock city. Symbolically, a drunken mob smashes it to smithereens. So much for the "Century of Progress."

CHARACTER DEVELOPMENT

The many characters in *The Old Bunch* are distinctly drawn, even as Levin skips from one story to another. All the youngsters receive fine educations in keeping with Jewish respect for learning. Most of the men make their way out of the ghetto through their professional achievements. Levin attempted to give all of his young characters equal treatment, but two idealistic men stand out as being the most complex. Sam Eisen represents Levin's position that one may be a nonbeliever, but still respect one's cultural identity. Sam does so despite the tide of irreverent assimilation he sees engulfing his contemporaries, including his girlfriend and wife-to-be, Lil, whom he eventually divorces because of her insensitivity. Sam is one of the few in the young group who does not denigrate his immigrant parents. He becomes a liberal lawyer and a supporter of unpopular radical causes. He idealistically defends the poor and downtrodden and is often bloodied but never broken by the corrupt legal system.

Joe Freedman, the sculptor, carries a torch for the only woman he ever loves, Sylvia Abramson, but he loses her to his friend Mitch Wilner, because he never can bring himself to commit to marriage even when he is succeeding professionally. As a result his personal life will always be bitter. Freedman comes close to Levin's early and historically significant concept that Jews can and should coalesce around a nationalistic endeavor: Zionism and the possibility of a Jewish homeland in Palestine.

After studying art at the University of Chicago, Joe journeys to Paris where he comes under the influence of Aaron Polansky, a sculptor whose subject is the Hebrew Bible. Joe then goes to Poland in order to visit the village in which his grandfather was born. There he meets young Jews who scorn the idea of emigrating to America. Instead it is to the ancestral Jewish land in Palestine that they will go. Joe continues his journey of self-discovery by journeying to Palestine and working on a Kibbutz prior to returning to Chicago to continue his artistic career. Joe's fictional progress is a replication of Meyer Levin's youth.

Athletics are symbolized by Sol Meisel, who becomes a professional bicycle racer. Like careers in law, medicine, and business, a successful sports career is also a way to prestige in *The Old Bunch*. Sol's wins and losses are one of the architectonic devices that hold the novel together.

Sol's teenage girlfriend, Estelle Green, is beautiful, gentle, and totally committed to their relationship, but they make the mistake of engaging in premarital sex. It is the first experience for both, and she incorrectly thinks she has become pregnant. Unfortunately, Joe abandons her and begins a promiscuous sex life with women he meets on the bicycle tours. The heartbroken Estelle, no longer a virgin, thinks she is now unworthy of marriage, and as a result becomes a dissolute party girl passed on from man to man.

Mitch Wilner and Rudy Stone become physicians and are disillusioned by corruption in the medical profession. Mitch learns that surgeons will operate on patients who are not likely to survive because they will earn large fees by doing so. Rudy is denied a research position at the internationally famous Mayo Clinic in Rochester, Minnesota, because he is Jewish. He and other young idealistic physicians try to open a medical cooperative clinic to minister to the poor in the Depression only to find themselves labeled as quacks, blackballed by the medical association, and denied access to Chicago hospitals. Later the radical doctors find that as the World's Fair is about to open, a leading hotel has cases of amoebic dysentery. They expect that the Chicago Health Department will announce a quarantine, but that would hurt business, and the fair at all costs must proceed unhindered by medical ethics and government responsibility for public safety. Mitch and Rudy suffer for their altruism and naïve faith in their profession.

In growing up in early twentieth-century Chicago, all young men intent on professional lives in medicine, law, or business must accommodate themselves to a capitalistic society that thrives on dishonest politics, deception, bribery, and sometimes violence.

Of the eight women members of the old bunch, it is only Sylvia Abramson who is able to influence the men who surround and overwhelm the women in the novel. She uses her intelligence to gain their respect, while her strong personality is a force in the direction of the group. She alone of the young women is not primarily invested in wondering about how far to go with boys, fearing pregnancy, fixating on courtship and marriage, and pushing their husbands toward material success.

THEMES

The Old Bunch is not a novel about the success of second generation Americans; it is a story of defeat, even as an entire generation of Americans were defeated by the failure of capitalism in the Great Depression of the 1930s. Some escape and survive; some are badly bruised by the compassionless system; others suffer and are coarsened or ground down by the weight of economic failings. No individual has control of his or her fate. Indeed, the individuals in the novel are to an extent submerged in the flow of history as Levin, a socialist, posits Marxist "scientific" determinism as the provider of personal fate.

A major theme in *The Old Bunch* is the archetypal struggle between generations. The traditional religious practices and values brought by Eastern European Jews to America are atrophying. Secular Americanism is an unstoppable force destroying Jewish consciousness in youth growing up in a vast metropolis. Levin is more sympathetic with the older ways. He sadly describes sacrilegious parodies of Jewish services, as when an assimilated mother holds a Passover service and invites gentile friends to have fun at it. A cake—not allowed at Passover—is served, as is ham, a forbidden meat. On another occasion a pompous rabbi in a full dress suit officiates at a lavish wedding, symbolic of gross, conspicuous consumption.

Without nostalgia, Levin realistically portrays the irreversible urbanization of a people who began life in the villages and small towns of Eastern Europe, but within two generations became the consummate American city dwellers. The children of immigrants have little use for the rigidity and puritanism of Orthodox Judaism. The young protagonists give up their Jewish names: Gittel becomes Ethel and Shulamith becomes Sylvia. However, when the young men and women begin to have children of their own, they look over their shoulders at their living parents and, fearing disapproval, they consider giving their children two names: a Jewish-sounding name for the grandparents and American names for themselves and to facilitate their children's assimilation. Levin's thematic depiction of American acculturation by Jewish immigrants and their offspring, and of the rapid abandonment of traditional Jewish values and practices, inspired later Jewish American fiction writers, such as Philip Roth, to do the same.

NARRATIVE STYLE

The Old Bunch is a carefully constructed, naturalistic group novel. It has no single narrative voice. The group, the "Bunch," is the collective main character. This naturalistic novel has no center. The point of view is that of the youths as they mature. A traditional plot with exposition, complications, and closure is absent. Instead, the interwoven experiences of individual characters create the patterned garment that is the novel. Like vessels, each character attempts to survive in the roaring mainstream of life in their America.

Levin is excellent with dialogue. The older generation uses Yiddish speech patterns and expressions, while the speech of the young people employs the patterns and slang words of the Jazz Age. Ultimately, Levin's narrative style followed the literary stylistic breakthrough of John Dos Passos in the *USA* trilogy (*The 42 Parallel* [1930], *1919* [1932], and *The Big Money* [1933]), where Dos Passos created what he called the "interpolated life story," a bundling of biographies into a long narrative that explores the role of individuals in the economic flow of American society.

The great virtues of *The Old Bunch* are its mastery of detail and its brilliantly accurate depiction of Chicago in the years between the two world wars of the twentieth century. In that respect, the novel is like James Joyce's depiction of Dublin in *Ulysses* (1922). Instead of a single Jewish central character ranging over a city—Dublin—in a single day as in *Ulysses*, *The Old Bunch* has a score of Jewish characters roaming Chicago over a period of 13 years.

HISTORICAL CONTEXT

Levin wrote *The Old Bunch* shortly after the Chicago World's Fair closed in the months from early 1935 through late 1936. The author was approximately the same age as the members of the old bunch, and, of course, he had lived through the historical events he has his characters learning about, talking about, or experiencing. Events and references to celebrities of the 1920s and 1930s inform the novel, allowing Levin to create a documentary structure while providing an authentic flavor for the text. Certain events are recorded in order to establish the historical context of the novel. In 1921 Levin notes that the great opera singer Enrico Caruso dies, while the heavyweight boxing champion Jack Dempsey beats the Frenchman Georges Carpentier. In 1923 the great Teapot Dome scandal of the Harding administration is brought to light, and the government is shown to be corrupted by presidential cronies. The focus in 1924 is on the infamous Nathan Leopold and Richard Loeb murder case that Levin later writes about in *Compulsion*. The talk of 1926 is the premature death of the silent movie romantic star, Rudolph Valentino. Charles A. Lindberg's solo nonstop flight to Paris is the top news story of 1927.

Of course, in 1929 the Stock Market Crash is the watershed event in the novel. Along with most of the American people, the economic status of the old bunch and their parents goes into a tailspin. Also, in Palestine, Arabs inflict a pogrom on Jewish agricultural settlers, and Zionism enters the novel. The year 1931 is established by reference to the deaths of World War I French General Joseph Joffre and Thomas Edison. The signifying event of 1932 is the shocking kidnapping of the Lindberg baby. That same year Franklin Delano Roosevelt wins the presidential election. He is inaugurated in January 1933, after surviving an assassination attempt.

In 1933 the Nazi Party takes control of the Reichstag, and Hitler becomes Chancellor of Germany. He begins the persecution of German Jews. The Chicago Jews are wondering where the German Jews will flee to as emigration to the United States is severely restricted, and Palestine is not feasible because of violent Arab hostility. Roosevelt prevents a meltdown of the U.S. financial structure by ordering a bank "holiday," and the American people are temporarily without cash. For a brief period the people of Chicago and all other Americans are reduced to bartering and buying on credit to survive. Finally, the Chicago World's Fair closes in 1934 as the novel concludes.

Levin salts the texts with references to, or appearances of, the movers and shakers of the 1920s and 1930s. Political greats include the Prince of Wales (later, briefly, King Edward the Eighth), Mahatma Gandhi, Emma Goldman the anarchist, and Benito Mussolini. Albert Einstein visits the Chicago Fair. The great architects Frank Lloyd Wright and Le Corbusier are mentioned. The artists Pablo Picasso, Claude Monet, Man Ray, Jean Cocteau, and Rockwell Kent are referred to. Henry Ford is given his due.

Sports greats besides Dempsey include the boxers Max Schmelling (Hitler's favorite), Max Baer (the Jewish heavy-weight champion), and Benny Leonard (the Jewish light-weight champion). Babe Ruth is depicted hitting a home run. Other sports figures include Red Grange the football phenomenon and the champion golfer Bobby Jones.

Movie stars included, besides Valentino, are Mae West, Gloria Swanson, Katharine Hepburn, Edward G. Robinson, Greta Garbo, Jean Harlow, and Harpo Marx. The popular composer Irving Berlin comes up. Singers and entertainers spoken of are Sophie Tucker, Eddie Cantor, Rudy Vallée, George Jessel, and the greatest entertainer of the period, Al Jolson. The historical figures in *The Old Bunch* produce a sense of currency in the novel and make the novel a virtual *Who's Who* of the years between the two world wars.

SUGGESTED READINGS

Primary Sources

Levin, Meyer. *In Search: An Autobiography.* New York: Horizon, 1950.
———. *The Old Bunch.* Secaucus, N.J.: Citadel, 1985.
———. *The Obsession.* New York: Simon & Schuster, 1973.

Secondary Source

Rubin, Joel. *Meyer Levin.* Boston: Twayne, 1982.

6

Saul Bellow
The Adventures of Augie March
(1953)

The Adventures of Augie March was Saul Bellow's third and breakthrough novel. It brashly announced a brand new voice in American fiction: jazzy and exuberant, with accents that are Midwestern American, urban, and Yiddish. It is an old-fashioned, episodic, long novel with larger-than-life characters, big themes, and important ideas. It is a post-World War II literary effort written for an America that was expanding in power and wealth and that had embraced consumerism and materialism. Furthermore, it is a Chicago kind of work: broad-shouldered, tough, pushy, and picaresque, like its predecessor novel, Meyer Levin's *The Old Bunch*. These qualities and its flowing prose brought it the 1954 National Book Award and established the writer as one of America's major younger authors of the time.

After this initial masterpiece, Bellow—who saw himself as a social historian examining the darkly comic struggles of his characters in their attempt to find meaning in life—would go on to greatness. For many critics and readers, the big three of Jewish American fiction writers are Saul Bellow, Bernard Malamud, and Philip Roth. But it was Bellow who received the Nobel Prize for Literature in 1976.

BIOGRAPHICAL CONTEXT

Saul Bellow, a truly American writer, was born Solomon Bellow in Lachine, Quebec, a suburb of Montreal inhabited by poor immigrants, on either June or

July 10, 1915. His Jewish parents did not use the Christian calendar and other records are not clear, but Bellow celebrated his birthday in June. He was the last of the four children of Abraham and Liza (Lescha) Gordin Bellow who had emigrated from Russia two years before Bellow's birth. Solomon was the first to be born in the New World. Abram (as his family called him) and Liza had had a difficult time in Russia, but life was not all that much better in Canada. Abram failed at one enterprise after another. Liza was a deeply religious woman who wanted her youngest child to become a rabbi, or at least a concert violinist. In 1923, when Bellow was eight years old, he became seriously ill, and he spent six months in the Royal Victoria Hospital, suffering from a severe respiratory infection. There the child became an avid reader, devouring anything printed.

The next year Abram moved the family across the border to Chicago, and life got a little easier as Abram found various jobs including work in a bakery, delivering coal, and bootlegging during Prohibition. The family remained religious. Young Bellow was steeped in Jewish tradition, but after a while, he began to rebel against the strictures of Orthodox Judaism as he joined other children of poor Jewish tailors, grocers, and peddlers who were reading and enjoying books in English borrowed from the public library. Furthermore, teeming Chicago with all its raw vitality was fascinating to the young man. The city would remain central to Bellow's literary work for many years to come.

Bellow began to write in elementary school and continued in Tuley High School from which he graduated in 1933. Abram thought Solomon was wasting his time. Liza was more supportive, but she died in 1932 while Bellow was still in high school. Bellow deeply mourned his mother. Abram remarried rather quickly and that too upset the youth, who now felt simultaneously dispossessed and liberated.

In 1933 Bellow enrolled in the University of Chicago, but two years later he transferred to Northwestern, because it was less expensive. He intended to study literature, but the anti-Semitic English Department made it clear that Jews were not equipped to study English literature, and so Bellow studied anthropology and sociology. He received a B.S. with honors in 1937. At Northwestern Bellow wrote stories for the campus literary magazine. It was then that he changed his first name to Saul. After Northwestern, Bellow began graduate work in anthropology at the University of Wisconsin. However, Bellow's heart was not in his studies; he really wanted to be a professional writer, and so he quit his graduate studies at Wisconsin after only a few months. He quickly got some Depression-era work on the W.P.A. Federal Writers' Project in Chicago, preparing biographies of Midwestern novelists. Then he was hired by the editorial department of the *Encyclopaedia Britannica* to work on Mortimer Adler's popular "Great Books" series.

Inevitably, Bellow made his way to New York's Greenwich Village as the 1930s came to an end. There he felt free to pursue the craft of fiction writing, while earning some money as a book reviewer. At the onset of World War II Bellow was rejected for military service because of a hernia. However, he joined the merchant marine and was in training when the war ended. During that period, he wrote and published his first novel, *Dangling Man* (1944), about the alienation of a young Chicagoan who is kicking around the city trying to find himself while waiting to be drafted. Bellow then taught at the University of Minnesota from 1946 to 1948.

Dangling Man was followed by *The Victim* (1947), a madcap novel that deals with Jewish guilt, anti-Semitism, and the barriers between gentiles and Jews. These first two novels were Bellow's apprenticeship efforts. Financed by a Guggenheim fellowship in 1948, Bellow went to Paris, where, while walking the streets of Paris, he thought of a childhood friend who was a wild talker and schemer. From this reminiscing came *The Adventures of Augie March* (1953), Bellow's first masterpiece, a National Book Award winner, and a best-seller. The novel is a satiric, picaresque bildungsroman—a story of maturation, growth, and education. The same year, 1953, Bellow translated Isaac Bashevis Singer's famous story "Gimpel the Fool" from Yiddish into English.

While teaching English at Princeton University and then Bard College, Bellow wrote the novella *Seize the Day* (1956). Because of its theme of alienation and the foolishness of striving for riches, it is considered by critics to be a small jewel of fiction. Bellow's next novel, *Henderson the Rain King* (1959), is the story of the spiritual journey of an American millionaire in Africa.

Bellow returned to Chicago in 1962 and joined the faculty of the University of Chicago. *Herzog* (1964), the story of a university professor's struggle to understand and come to terms with a patently unjust world, won a second National Book Award. *Mr. Sammler's Planet* (1970), for which Bellow won his third National Book Award, focuses on the urban unrest of the late 1960s as seen by a Holocaust survivor living in New York City.

Humboldt's Gift (1975) received the Pulitzer Prize for Literature. It is the story of a self-destructive poet's demise (based on the life of Bellow's friend, the troubled poet Delmore Schwartz) and the limited authority of the artist in a materialistic society.

In 1967 Bellow had journeyed to Israel to report on the Six Day War. He saw that for the second time in less than a quarter of a century hundreds of thousands of Jews had guns pointed at them. Bellow was deeply moved by the courage of the Israeli people, and he remained committed to the new country and Jewish haven for the rest of his life. In 1975 he spent a three-month sabbatical lecturing at the Hebrew University in Jerusalem, from which came his most important nonfiction book, *To Jerusalem and Back: A Personal Account* (1976), a highly sophisticated portrait of the problems in the Middle East.

After the Nobel award in 1976, Bellow produced two shorter unsuccessful novels, short stories, and failed plays. *Ravelstein* (2000), a return to long fiction, revived Bellow's reputation. It was inspired by the life of his friend Allan Bloom, the social critic and author of *The Closing of the American Mind*. *Ravelstein* is a story of male friendship; it focuses on a brilliant and celebrated professor who is dying of AIDS.

In 1993, after many years of living in Chicago and teaching at the University of Chicago, Bellow left his adopted city and moved to Boston. Boston University's chancellor, John Silber, had offered him a lucrative academic appointment, and he accepted it. The reasons for his departure were complex, but clearly Chicago held sad memories because several of Bellow's close friends had recently died. Also, he was bothered by the ugly racial climate in the Windy City at the time.

Bellow was married five times. His wives were Anita Goshkin, Alexandra Tsachacbasov, Susan Glassman, Alexandra Ionescu Tulcea, and Janis Freedman. All the marriages but his last ended in divorce. He had three sons and a daughter. Saul Bellow died in his home in Brookline, Massachusetts in 2005.

PLOT DEVELOPMENT

The Adventures of Augie March is an exuberant comedy with dark overtones, reflecting the high value given to making fun of the human condition found in Yiddish literature. Bellow launches Augie out of his painful, impoverished childhood in Chicago. A poor, simple-minded, weak-willed, nearly blind Rebecca March, along with her three sons—Simon, Augie, and George—has been abandoned by her husband. The household is dominated by a controlling, elderly Russian Jewish woman boarder, a self-appointed "grandmother," who wants "to make something" out of Augie and his older brother, Simon. Sadly, Grandma Lausch is responsible for committing the mentally handicapped George to an institution, an act that causes the sympathetic Augie much pain, regret, and guilt.

Augie's childhood world is terrifying. He is often beaten. On one occasion, because he is a Jew, he is beaten up by Christian punks, including one who supposedly was his friend.

Augie pays little attention to school, partly because the family needs income from Simon and him to survive. It's the jobs the teenager finds that introduce him to a world where hustling and thieving flourish, and he too becomes a petty thief. Soon he is a companion, aide, servant, male nurse, and courtier to William Einhorn, the paraplegic ruler of a section of West Side Chicago. Then he is made a pet by a North Shore matron, Mrs. Renling, wife of his employer in a clothing store. People think he is her gigolo, while she would like to adopt the affable and handsome young man. He refuses. When Simon March marries Charlotte Magnus, a wealthy woman, Augie becomes his aide. He is set to marry Charlotte's younger sister, Lucy, but loses the "golden" opportunity when he tries to help a pregnant young friend and is wrongly perceived as the father.

In the middle of the novel Augie is beaten up again, this time because he is a union organizer in a labor strike. Thea, a wealthy, eccentric, young married woman whom he had met when he was squiring Mrs. Renling, comes back into his life. They fall in love, and she talks him into going to Mexico.

The climactic episode of the novel occurs in Mexico where Augie, Thea, and her pet American eagle have gone to hunt giant iguanas that they could sell to zoos. The mad scheme fails, of course. Augie suffers a concussion that takes weeks to mend, and he falls into depression. Thea is controlling, and he is passive. As Augie tries to help Stella, an actress who is running away from her husband, he finds himself stuck on a mountain with her. He goes to seek aid. It is night, and he does not know if he is seeing stars or lights from human habitation. Awed by the sight of the eternal heavens, he has an epiphany. It is a significant moment of self-realization: he needs stillness to endure and survive. He returns to Stella and makes love with her, thus freeing himself from the power of Thea.

Having replaced Thea in Augie's affections, Stella waits for Augie in New York City where they eventually marry while he has trained to serve in the wartime Merchant Marine. Shipping out on convoy duty, Augie survives the torpedoing of his vessel, only to come close to being killed in a lifeboat by an insane fellow survivor. Reunited after the war, Augie and Stella go to Paris where Stella has film-acting commitments in Paris.

In Paris Augie realizes that Stella has prospects and perspectives of her own. But Augie refuses to live a disappointed, tag-along life. He will seek comfort and quiet in the unknown vistas that will unfold before him in solitary travels. He must explore and move on, escaping from those who would exert power over him, as he seeks the stillness his mind and his soul crave. Although he is still not sure if he will ever truly find himself, he can at least recount the tales of his youthful adventures. Augie March, almost alone of Bellow's heroes, continually slips from the clutches of those who try to control him and escapes the ravages of a cruel and destructive world.

CHARACTER DEVELOPMENT

Augie March is a morally, intellectually, and emotionally extravagant character, surely larger than life. He is tough, sensitive, and handsome, but he is also Jewish, fatherless, and broke: great disadvantages in the early twentieth century if not at any time. He is a nonhero, an existentialist individual who does not commit; an operator and a hustler who is more taken advantage of by his brother, employers, and girlfriends than he takes advantage of others. Tolerant and affectionate, he is frequently swept up in the enthusiasms of others. In fact, he is often trying to get out of the grasp of manipulative and exploitive people. Thus we can sympathize with him even when he does wrong. Augie, like Voltaire's Candide, never shares his author's sardonic view of humanity. On the contrary, he is an uncalculating enthusiast easily swept up by those about whom he cares, but one who always survives.

Augie's preoccupations fluctuate between the active world and the world of thought. Again, like Voltaire's Candide, he learns that humans are good and evil, and in that respect no one is really better than anyone else. He also comes to understand that the world is full of trouble and danger that cannot be ignored or avoided, so laugh at them if one can. As in much Yiddish literature, relief, if not hope, is found in laughter.

Augie's occupations include: burglar, would-be illegal immigrant smuggler, clothing salesman, labor union organizer, book thief, dog minder, eagle trainer, wartime merchant marine seaman, and shady go-between in illegal importing. Augie's adventures include a cross-country escapade riding the rails on a boxcar, working in his brother's coal yard, a summer in Mexico, being torpedoed at sea, a transatlantic voyage, and a romantic self-exile in post–World War II Paris.

Augie is questing for enduring love and a meaningful vocation, but he does not quite find them. Yet his life is not totally unsuccessful: he has good friends, he delights in sensuality, and he is happy to be alive. Like any normal person, he compromises. Augie's love life reads like an adolescent fantasy. His girlfriends are many and varied. Lucy Magnus is a stereotypical, frigid rich girl who is selfishly calculating. Mimi, the waitress always in trouble, is the frank, good-natured pal type, and so Augie does not make love to her. Sophie, the good-natured hotel chambermaid and labor union organizer, is not interesting enough to hold Augie. The rich and beautiful Thea chases Augie, who was first in love with her sister, Esther. Thea loves him passionately and is glad to support him in Mexico, until she tires of him and departs, leaving Augie seemingly broken-hearted. However, his pain is short-lived and assuaged in the arms of Stella, the movie actress who becomes his wife and with whom he moves to Europe as the novel nears conclusion.

Grandma Lausch, a cynical Jewish matriarch, who is actually not Augie's grandmother, raises Augie while his mother is going blind. Lausch hopes that he will grow up to be something like her vision of a Russian gentleman. Young Augie is in awe of her power. She represents the very old-world culture Augie is fleeing. She tries to teach Augie to be ruthless and impersonal. Her fate is to be treated impersonally by her real sons who abandon her in a nursing home when she is old and ill.

Augie's brother, Simon, unlike Augie, is madly searching for money and power even though he starts out as an idealistic youth. Unlike Augie, Simon is corrupted by the American male dream of accumulation: material goods, property, and women. As, symbolically, he grows fatter and fatter, much of the rest of his life is devoted to making money and seducing women as well as impressing his younger brother with whom he has always had a love–hate relationship.

The villainous William Einhorn, the intelligent, self-educated wheelchair-bound political boss, runs Chicago's Thirteenth Ward. He rules that fiefdom like a medieval duke. He is a cynical, clever, lecherous old man for whom Augie works as an errand boy, private nurse, and wheelchair pusher. Vicious as Einhorn is, Augie nevertheless is able to see some good in him. In fact, Augie, like Candide, can see something redeeming in everyone.

Thea represents freedom, adventure, and abandonment. She takes Augie from his natural environment—Chicago—into the wider world. Caligula, the eagle, with whom Thea intends to capture iguanas, is the external symbol of her power. Caligula preys, must continually be groomed and served, and is dangerous. Augie must extricate himself from Thea's control if he is ever to have a normal equal relationship with a woman.

Many more interesting and well-drawn characters come and go in the richness of Bellow's long, highly imaginative text.

THEMES

A pervading theme in *The Adventures of Augie March* is the transformative power of American optimism as symbolized by the eponymous character. American life is full of vitality. Augie is a can-do American, even in dire times. He is imbued with the American spirit of adventure and the belief in tomorrow. Like a movie cowboy, he won't conform, even if conforming would bring him wealth and power. When he comes to understand himself, he is satisfied and even happy. Bellow touts the American dream like an evangelist. It's a faith. It can be sustained, despite evidence of its unreality, as long as one is stubborn enough.

Another theme in the novel is the fluidity of American society to the point that the American is constantly seeking his or her identity as if it were something lost. Bellow implies that in an ultra-mobile society the chameleon-like personality is best fitted to survive, or at least have the most fun.

An easily recognized American theme in the novel is the struggle of the individual against a controlling, materialistic society. Augie is a restless, stubborn nonconformist whose travelogue life symbolizes the restlessness of the American.

The Adventures of Augie March is a morality tale about the individual failure of ideals and how it is better to carry on like Augie. He has respect for his fellow humans. He does not live with a low opinion of others. He keeps his individuality. He is hopeful, not deterministic. He examines his life honestly. He refuses to be trapped in relationships, ideologies, or "isms." In these ways he is a primitive American or a nineteenth-century American idealist like Emerson or Thoreau. Bellow has Augie advocate love and charity. The author and his alter ego love life even as they pity the human condition. But Augie March cannot humanize a terrible world, of course, and that is the cause of his ultimate winding down.

NARRATIVE STYLE

The Adventures of Augie March is an episodic, first-person, memoir-like novel full of high-culture allusions written ostensibly by a man in his early forties, who is married and living in self-imposed exile in France long after the events of his life he is describing, and who has auto-didactically received enough education through the compulsive reading of great works of literature and philosophy to appreciate his experiences in symbolic and metaphysical terms. Bellow builds his stylistically free-wheeling novel of a Candide-like innocent—minus much virtue—with bricks of references to all of Western literature, philosophy, and history while continually surprising and entertaining the informed reader with startling analogies. Bellow incorporates famous myths and legends. Augie is a wandering Jew accepting, affirming, and devouring all of American and European culture. Bellow has set loose a wild youth upon a grand stage, and he gives that young man free range to observe, experience, and overcome a battalion of Machiavellians bent on using him.

Augie's bildungsroman saga typhoons out of the early-twentieth century Chicago of his childhood, down to Mexico, onto the Atlantic Ocean, and across to Europe. In the end, however, as the stormy memoir winds down, Augie, older and wiser perhaps, is still a Columbus scanning the horizon.

HISTORICAL CONTEXT

The Adventures of Augie March is initially set in the raucous, energetic, materialistic Chicago of the late 1920s and the Depression era. It is the same environment and time period that Meyer Levin employed in *The Old Bunch*. In 1929, when Augie is 14, Herbert Hoover is the president and the stock market crashes. The Great Depression follows.

Bellow places his hero in a world that is beset with too much history. The Nazis are growing in strength in Germany as the 1930s commence. The economy of the United States is crippled. American veterans of World War I march on Washington trying to force Congress to pay them a promised bonus. Under orders of the president, General Douglas MacArthur drives them from the city and burns the shanties of men who had served with him in the war. But the people find renewed hope with the election of Franklin Delano Roosevelt to the presidency in 1932. Still bread lines in cities like Chicago and New York are long. Twenty-five percent of the work force is unemployed. Strikes are brutally repressed by strike-breakers, police, and national guardsmen.

The nation drifts closer and closer to the Left as the Communist Party of America is at its strongest point in history. Some of Augie's friends are communists. At one point Augie nearly becomes the secretary to Stalin's arch-enemy Leon Trotsky, the great communist revolutionary in exile in Mexico. Trotsky is assassinated in Mexico City by the order of Stalin in 1940. Bellow continually projects Augie into the historical world just as Meyer Levin did with his characters in *The Old Bunch*.

When World War II breaks out, Augie tries to enlist in the army and the navy but is rejected because he is not physically fit enough. He does manage to train for the Merchant Marine, ship out, get torpedoed, and survive a long, dangerous drift in a lifeboat with a mad companion. Rescued, he continues in the war by serving on merchant ships in three more Atlantic crossings. As a veteran, he wants peace that is not to be found in bustling American cities, but in war-damaged and war weary Paris where the lights have gone on again. The exhausted quiet of post-war Europe is the final background of the novel.

SUGGESTED READINGS

Primary Sources

Bellow, Saul. *The Adventures of Augie March*. New York: Viking, 1953.
———. *To Jerusalem and Back: A Personal Memoir*. New York: Viking, 1976.

Secondary Sources

Atlas, James. *Bellow: A Biography*. New York: Random House, 2001.
Bradbury, Malcolm. *Saul Bellow*. New York: Methuen, 1982.
Hyland, Peter. *Saul Bellow*. New York: St. Martin's, 1992.
Kiernan, Robert F. *Saul Bellow*. New York: Continuum, 1989.

7

Bernard Malamud
The Assistant
(1957)

The Assistant is a brilliant but melancholy novel about what it is to be a Jew. It explores the dark realm of pathos in a world where the past is bleak and the future seems to hold no promise. It can be read as a moral allegory, stating that human beings can endure the instability of their world as well as great psychological and physical agony when they have an inner strength based on ingrained values. Indeed, *The Assistant* pays tribute to the redeeming power of love—familial, sexual, and spiritual—to light up even the most drab existence in the bleakest of environs.

BIOGRAPHICAL CONTEXT

Bernard Malamud was born in Brooklyn, New York, in 1914, the son of Max and Bertha Fidelman Malamud. Both had come from Russia in the early 1900s. Max was a grocer who barely made a living for his family. Although Bertha was a warm and loving mother, Max was a crude and caustic husband and father. During Malamud's childhood the Malamuds moved from neighborhood to neighborhood. A second child, Eugene, was born in 1917. At the age of nine Bernard contracted pneumonia. When he was well, as a recovery gift, Max bought the 20 volumes of the *Book of Knowledge* for his son, although the family could hardly afford it. It made the boy an inveterate reader.

Malamud's mother's family had Yiddish actors and theater folk in it, and he was taken to plays on the Lower East Side's Second Avenue, the Yiddish Broadway, long before he saw a Broadway show. Bertha was unhappy in her marriage. She slowly became schizophrenic. When she tried to kill herself by drinking a household disinfectant, she was rescued by Malamud and the neighborhood pharmacist, but she spent the rest of her life in a mental institution, dying in 1929. Eugene became mentally unstable after army service. Psychiatry did not help, and after an unproductive life, he died in 1974.

With his mother's death Malamud went to work in the grocery store after school and on weekends. It was then he began to write. He attended Erasmus Hall High School, where his writing was encouraged. Some nights he stayed on in the back room of the store when it was closed, working on stories. At Erasmus Hall he was editor of the literary magazine. In 1932 Malamud entered City College of New York from which he received a bachelor's degree in 1936, after which he worked at various jobs including shop assistant, factory worker, and in 1940 as a clerk in the Census Bureau in Washington, D.C. He continued to write stories.

Malamud began an M.A. at Columbia University in 1938, while working at Erasmus as a night school teacher. He lived in a furnished room for many years while studying at Columbia, teaching at night and always honing the writer's craft. He received his M.A. degree in 1942.

Malamud married Ann de Chiara in 1945. They had two children: Paul, born in New York City in 1947, and Janna, born in Corvallis, Oregon, in 1952. The latter published a memoir of her father in 2006 (see "Suggested Readings" at the end of this chapter). In 1949 Malamud moved the family to Corvallis, Oregon, where he taught English at Oregon State College. In the dozen years there—minus a year in Italy on a *Partisan Review* fellowship (1956–1957)—his stories began to appear in major periodicals. More significantly, in those 12 years, he published his first four long works of fiction—three novels and a short story collection—and made his reputation as a major American writer.

Malamud's first published novel, *The Natural* (1952), is the story of the rise and fall of a superb baseball player who is unable to bridle his passions. Surprisingly, the novel has no Jewish characters in it. Malamud's next novel, *The Assistant* (1957), the realistic story of the sad life and trials of a poor, endlessly suffering Jewish grocer like his father, carried him into the first rank of Jewish American writers. *The Assistant* is widely considered Malamud's masterpiece.

The first collection of Malamud's stories, *The Magic Barrel* (1958), received the National Book Award a year after publication. *A New Life* (1961), a novel, is the story of S. Levin, a 30-year-old failure seeking a new life by leaving New York and going to teach at a philistine, agricultural cow college in the

Pacific Northwest, and who finds redemption in an improbable love affair with a married woman with children. In 1961 Malamud left Oregon to move back East and teach at Bennington College in Vermont. He also obtained an apartment in New York City.

Idiots First (1963) was Malamud's second collection of short stories. In 1965 Malamud traveled in the Soviet Union, France, and Spain. The most complex of Malamud's novels, *The Fixer* (1966), is based on the actual case of Mendel Beiliss, a Russian Jew wrongly accused of the ritual murder of a Christian boy in Kiev, Ukraine, in 1913, but acquitted despite the strength of the anti-Semitic conspiracy against him. *The Fixer* depicts the similar ordeal of a poor Jewish man, Yokav Bok, who has left the ghetto, pretending to be a Christian in order to find work, and whose identity is discovered when a Christian boy is murdered. Bok is wrongly charged with ritual murder. The rest of the book deals with the anti-Semitic investigation and trial of a philosophical man who will not confess despite torture and humiliation. *The Fixer* received the Pulitzer Prize and Malamud's second National Book Award.

Pictures of Fidelman: An Exhibition (1969) contains six stories brought together as a picaresque novel portraying the adventures of an American art student in Italy, a schlemiel who tries to find himself in his work, but life gets in his way. *The Tenants* (1971) is a flawed novel that illustrates the agony of creative activity as two writers, one a black man and the other a Jew, living in a condemned tenement on Manhattan's East Side, proceed from good will and respect to territorial, literary, and sexual conflict. *Rembrandt's Hat* (1973) contains eight stories in which Malamud expresses compassionate concern about how external bonds can tie two people together even though they continually fail to communicate with each other. *Dubin's Lives* (1979) is about a 56-year-old professional biographer who lives the lives of others by writing them, but is tempted to disregard his real responsibilities to his marriage because of his attraction to a young, promiscuous woman.

God's Grace (1982) is an engrossing fantasy taking place after a worldwide nuclear conflict in which Calvin Cohn, a paleontologist, has escaped death by having worked under the sea on a research vessel while the total destruction of humanity takes place above. Like Robinson Crusoe, he adjusts to life on a desert island where miraculously some other primates—baboons, chimpanzees, and a gorilla whom Cohn names George and who becomes Cohn's "Man Friday"—have survived. The ultimate messages—vintage Malamud—are that love and compassion can bond humans and animals, and life is always better than death.

In 1982 Malamud underwent heart bypass surgery and suffered a stroke on the operating table. He never fully recovered, and he died of a massive heart attack in New York City in 1986.

PLOT DEVELOPMENT

The world of *The Assistant* is a tiny, fated world, a Greek tragedy on a stage. It is set on a small street with a few shops and a subway station in a mixed gentile and Jewish working-class neighborhood in Brooklyn. It is not clear if the time is the Great Depression or the immediate post-World War II period, but the projected atmosphere of hopelessness is overtly Depression-tinged. Morris and Ida Bober, a middle-aged couple, run a failing grocery store. Their only hope is to sell the store, but there are no buyers. Their daughter, Helen, an attractive woman in her mid-twenties and their only child, helps keep the family financially afloat by contributing a large part of her salary from her secretarial job. Morris, with Ida's help, works very long hours, seven days a week, to stay in business. The small family is a microcosm of threatened, vulnerable humanity, doomed to be swept along helplessly and ultimately drowned in the economic storms that always engulf the poor.

One night, Morris, a good-hearted and credulous person, is warned by his annoying neighbor, Julius Karp, who owns the nearby successful liquor store, that two robbers are parked on the street. Karp, who is the intended target, locks up, but Morris does not, and the robbers choose him as the alternate victim. They find only a few dollars in the cash register, and so the more vicious thief hits Morris over the head with his pistol. He is incapacitated for a while, requiring Ida to run the store alone.

The second robber, Frank Alpine, an Italian American and a drifter who grew up in an orphanage, is remorseful. He comes back to the store and without revealing his part in the robbery, offers to help out in the grocery without pay, supposedly to learn the grocer's trade. His help is initially refused partly because he is not Jewish and the Bobers are suspicious of his motivation. Since he has no place to live and is running out of money, Frank hides in the store's cellar, and survives by stealing milk and bread daily. Appearing again, Frank is hired by the Bobers, because Morris is still too ill to work as he did before. Frank does well for the store, increasing the business. At first he is not paid, and then he is given very little, so he begins to steal small amounts. Also, he falls in love with the beautiful and sad Helen, who is recovering from a very brief affair with Nat Pearl, a Jewish law student from a more affluent family. She has broken with Nat because she is sure he only wants sex, while she wants marriage. She is also sad because she did not have the money to go to college and thus is trapped in a boring job.

Initially, Helen ignores Frank. He is not Jewish, and her parents would never consent to a marriage with a gentile anyway. Frank is possessed. He even climbs up a dumbwaiter shaft to spy on Helen in the bathroom of the family's flat above the store. Slowly, Helen comes to recognize that Frank is basically a good person, and she falls in love with him. However, they must meet secretly because the Bobers would be furious is they found out that there was something between their daughter and an uneducated, impoverished gentile drifter.

Frank wants to help Helen in every way including giving her a chance to go to college. He stops stealing while Morris is in the hospital with pneumonia and starts paying back the money he has stolen by adding to the register from his meager pay and small savings.

But the lovers are star-crossed. One day, Frank, now broke from returning money to the register, needs a dollar for carfare to meet Helen. He takes one dollar from the money he has put into the till, and Morris catches him and fires him. Morris had also learned that Frank and Helen have been seeing each other. In fact, they had made love. Later that night, when Helen arrived at a rendezvous site in a park where she is anticipating making love with Frank once more, she is raped by Frank's nemesis, Ward Minogue, the first robber. Frank appears too late to save Helen, but after seeing Helen with her clothing in disarray, he is unable to stop himself from taking advantage of her state. Helen is shocked, and now hates him for roughly forcing her.

Frank comes back to Morris to confess his part in the robbery, but Morris had figured that out in the hospital, and he can't forgive Frank. Sick with pneumonia and hospitalized, Morris again is unable to support his impoverished family, and although Ida refuses to let Frank open and run the store again, the distraught and heart-broken young man secretly does open the store and even takes a night job as a counterman in a restaurant to keep the shop afloat. The grateful Ida relents, and Frank is fully accepted back while still working at night.

Fate is malicious. When the drunken Minogue burns down the next-door liquor shop, killing himself in the act, Karp, the owner, offers to buy Morris's grocery at a generous price so that he can turn it into a liquor store. The family seems saved, but nemesis intervenes. Before the deal can be finalized, Morris foolishly shovels snow in the bitter cold, falls ill again, and dies in the hospital three days later. Shortly after the funeral, Ida, Helen, and Frank learn that Karp has had a heart attack and will never work again, and so the deal is off. Frank becomes the breadwinner once more, struggling day and night to support Ida and the grocery. Helen thanks him for his self-sacrificing, and the one-time drifter begins to learn Yiddish. He has himself circumcised, and becomes a Jew, partly in order to make himself acceptable to Helen in the hope that he could win her love once more, but also because he has come to understand the endurance and strength of the ever-suffering Jewish people. The orphan needs to become a part of a community and share its destiny.

CHARACTER DEVELOPMENT

Morris is a 60-year-old grocer from the Jewish ghetto on the Lower East Side of Manhattan, who now owns an obsolete store in a poor Brooklyn neighborhood. He is tormented by the fact that he is always on the brink of bankruptcy and almost unable to support his small family, a Jewish man's sacred duty. He must work 12-hour days, carrying milk crates that are too heavy for him, and dealing with the tormenting fact that competition from another store is killing his business. He must endure the nagging of Ida, his wife, about their poverty and his generosity to poor customers.

In many ways Morris is only superficially Jewish. He does not keep the Sabbath, he sells nonkosher products such as ham, and he never goes to synagogue. But Morris has a Jewish soul: he respects his wife, he is charitable, he forgives those like Frank and Karp who hurt him, and he has compassion for everyone who needs it. Morris's decent nature evokes sympathy in the reader, so that when he dies we share in the grief of the family, friends, and Frank.

Ida is 51 years old and tired of the life of a poor grocer's wife. Her feet hurt. She is permanently disgruntled, because when Morris married her, he took her from the comfort of a nearly all-Jewish community—presumably the Lower East Side—to the wilds of Brooklyn. She, on the other hand, denied Morris an alternative occupation to small businessperson when she insisted that he drop out of pharmacy school when they marry and immediately earn a living. Despite her nagging, Ida loves Morris and will tend the store as well as care for the flat when her husband is ill. Ida is deeply fearful for Helen. She wants her daughter to marry a well-off Jewish man as soon as possible. Ida is suspicious of Frank from the beginning. She is always prophesying doom and disaster. Ida, like a Cassandra, is usually right and always unheeded.

Frank, the point-of-view character, is a conflicted young man who lies, steals, and hates himself for it. He has a conscience and a sense of guilt, possibly because of his Roman Catholic upbringing in an orphanage. The orphan seems to be looking for a father, and he almost finds one in Morris, who had a son that died as a child. Frank is the one who changes most. He represents the skeptical gentile world encountering the Jewish world. When he falls passionately in love with the reluctant and depressed Helen, he continually fumbles, doing or saying the wrong thing. He tries to pay back Morris for having taken part in the robbery in which Morris was brutally pistol-whipped, by working himself to exhaustion in the store. Thus penitent, he expiates his guilt and finds purpose and hope in working for Morris's widow and Helen. As he has said to the Bobers all along: he is a good man.

Helen is a frustrated, disappointed, and depressed young woman. She had the ability to succeed in college, but was not given the chance. She holds a miserable job. She is rightly particular when it comes to men, but she would like to marry. Nat Pearl, a Jewish suitor acceptable to her parents, is more interested in sex than marrying this beautiful but poor girl. Her sexual frustration leads her to trouble. Frank interests her because he is different from the few men she has dated, and because she senses something decent in him. At the end, although she had come to detest him for losing control and taking advantage of her, she is moved by his contrition and may indeed eventually find a modicum of happiness as the wife of a convert to Judaism. Ironically, the only businesses Frank knows are groceries and take-out food joints. Is her husband-to-be a reincarnated Morris? And is she fated to become her mother?

THEMES

The modern existentialist credo is "I suffer, therefore I am." Suffering is a major theme in *The Assistant*. Although suffering is a basic human condition, it is, for Jews, what they seem to have been "chosen" for. They appear fated to suffer regardless of how they endeavor to avoid it. Morris is the epitome of Jewish suffering and, by extension, suffering humankind. He suffers for his principles and for the love of others. For Jews suffering is endemic even in Brooklyn. In part it is because they are perpetually seen as outsiders. Gentiles in the novel continually refer to Jews in a pejorative manner. Even though Morris opens up the store early in order to sell a Polish woman a daily roll for her breakfast, he is never thanked, but instead, he is treated to a hateful stare.

A concomitant theme to the theme of suffering is that of compassion. In fact, they are related. One's suffering provokes empathy and compassion for the pain of others, and a Jewish definition of what it is to be a decent human being is to have compassion. Although Morris is desperately afraid of losing the pitiful shop through bankruptcy, he initially ignores Frank's pilfering from the cash register, thinking compassionately that the poor drifter is only paid slave wages. A victim all his life, Morris cannot victimize another person.

Because Frank has been the partial cause of Morris's suffering, he has compassion for Morris from the time Morris is beaten, and Frank brought him a glass of water instead of running away. Frank's compassion for Morris grows when he realizes how much Morris suffered because of him. It is the first small step in his becoming a Jew. Malamud uses Jewishness as a metaphor for spiritual life. "Have mercy" is Malamud's distillation of Jewish ethics. He is rather less interested in religious or cultural qualities.

Love is yet another transcending theme in *The Assistant*. Frank, so alone, is desperately in need of love. It is through his love of Helen, and even of Morris, that he comes into his humanity. Helen treats love as a dangerous antagonist who can only hurt her and who does, while Ida's unspoken love for her husband and daughter raises her in the reader's perception from a droning scold to an appealing example of what a good heart will endure for the welfare of a family.

NARRATIVE STYLE

Malamud employs an omniscient narrator whose style of speaking is inflected as if he were a born Yiddish speaker now speaking English with the dialect of the Jewish comic. For example, when spring weather is awful, Morris asks as if translating from Yiddish: "What kind of winter can be in April?" The narrator employs ironic understatement in the face of pain, bad luck, and evil. Through him, Malamud skillfully lets the reader enter the minds of various characters as they reveal their hidden motivations and rationalize their errors and the harm they do.

In *The Assistant* Malamud is writing in the naturalist–realist tradition first brought into modern literature by late nineteenth-century French writers such as Gustave Flaubert and Émile Zola. At the same time, the novel is lyrical, symbolic, and ritualistic. The ritual conflict in a father–son relationship emerges because Morris and Frank are seekers: the former for a substitute for his dead son, and the latter for the father he never knew.

Symbolically, again and again, Frank thinks about St. Francis of Assisi, stories of whom he heard in the orphanage. It is St. Francis's dedication to poverty that, unconsciously, Frank and Morris ecumenically embrace. Morris and St. Francis have a gentleness that is Jewish and saintly Christian.

Frank's hanging around the grocery is his self-punishment for the crime he committed. Like the great nineteenth-century Russian novels of Tolstoy and

Dostoyevsky, *The Assistant*, primarily through the character of Frank, shows how human beings are capable of profound change.

Malamud uses ironic twists and bizarre occurrences that are commonplace in Yiddish literature. When Morris tries to burn down his grocery for the insurance money, he fails because the fire quickly goes out. He can make a fire, but can't get any ashes. Ironically, the drunken Minogue burns down the liquor store without even trying.

HISTORICAL CONTEXT

The Great Depression was an economic slump in North America, Europe, and other industrialized areas of the world, that began in 1929 with the catastrophic Stock Market Crash and lasted until late 1939, when Europe was in conflict and the United States was preparing for war. It was the longest and most severe depression ever experienced in the industrialized Western world. In America many thousands of investors were ruined, businesses failed by the thousands, almost one-third of American banks became insolvent, and unemployment was unprecedented. In 1932 one out of four American workers was out of work, while manufacturing fell by half.

In the same year the economic distress led to the election of Franklin D. Roosevelt as president. In the "New Deal" he introduced many progressive changes to the American economy, such as massive deficit government spending to stoke business and raise employment. In order to get hundreds of thousands back to work, Roosevelt created the Works Projects Administration, in which massive construction projects made work available for skilled and unskilled workers across the nation. Artists, musicians, writers, and actors found creative work. The Civilian Conservation Corp took 500,000 unemployed young men from the cities and put them to work planting some three billion trees, thus reforesting America.

City life was very hard during the Depression. Bread lines fed the hungry. Hundreds of thousands of small businesses failed. Jews like Malamud's parents struggled to feed their children. American anti-Semitism, which began to rise in the 1920s with racially motivated restrictions on immigration of people from Eastern Europe—where most Jews had come from—manifested itself in the denial of higher education to qualified Jewish youths in the major universities such as Harvard and Yale; in restrictions preventing Jewish Americans access to many hotels, resorts, clubs, and restaurants around the country; and the subjugating of Jews to an outpouring of hatred on the radio and in publications run by leading American figures such as the industrialist Henry Ford.

American Jews in the 1930s were also deeply worried for their co-religionists in Europe—relatives for some—where the Germans were embracing Hitler, Italians had become fascists, and violent anti-Semitism was on the rise in Poland, Hungary, and Romania, the 500-year-old home of millions of Yiddish-speaking Jews. With the revelation of the horrors of the German Holocaust after World War II, American Jews suffered deep depression as they mourned for the murder of six million of their co-religionists, and they felt guilt for not having done, or not having been able to do, more to prevent the German Holocaust, or help its victims.

The sorrow in *The Assistant* is a distillation of the Jewish grief, pain, and fear that informed the first 40 years of Bernard Malamud's life.

SUGGESTED READINGS

Primary Source

Malamud, Bernard. *The Assistant*. New York: Farrar, Straus & Giroux, 1957.

Secondary Sources

Abramson, Edward A. *Bernard Malamud Revisited*. New York: Twayne, 1993.

Helterman, Jeffrey. *Understanding Bernard Malamud*. Columbia: University of South Carolina Press, 1985.

Hershinow, Sheldon J. *Bernard Malamud*. New York: P. Unger, 1980.

Richman, Sidney. *Bernard Malamud*. New York: Twayne. 1970.

Smith, J. M. *My Father Is a Book: A Memoir of Bernard Malamud*. New York: Houghton Mifflin, 2006.

8

Chaim Potok
The Chosen
(1967)

The Chosen, a paean to friendship and life that ends with optimism, states that Jewish life goes on in America, and the succeeding young generations will be well prepared for success and leadership. The title, *The Chosen*, refers to the historic belief of the Jewish people that they are God's chosen people, chosen to bring monotheism to the world, as well as God's words and will through the Bible. They also believe that they were chosen to be "a light unto the nations": that is, to set standards for ethical and moral behavior and for the promulgation of justice and mercy.

Surely for many Jewish people the appellation "The Chosen People" is fraught with irony considering the long history of the persecution of the Jews throughout much of the world. Indeed, much of the chronological period of Potok's novel is the time of the Holocaust, the greatest disaster in Jewish history after the destruction of the Temple and the city of Jerusalem in 70 c.e. Yet the time of the novel also encompasses the return of the Jews, after nearly two thousand years of exile, to Israel, the land that God promised Moses would be their eternal homeland. Perhaps the Jews are the Chosen People after all?

BIOGRAPHICAL CONTEXT

Chaim Potok was a Jewish American philosopher, spiritual leader, professor, and most of all, a distinguished writer. Through his powerful narratives, Potok explored moral and ethical dilemmas while remaining committed to his belief in God. He was fascinated with the relationship between the Deity and the Jewish people. Potok was an affirmative writer. He believed that there is goodness in almost all people, and that life is precious, good, and very worth living. In presenting the cultural confrontation between traditional Jewish values and American material life in *The Chosen*, he offered the conclusion that American life is enriched by Jewishness. In return, Potok implied that American freedom, equality, and opportunity have given Jews the opportunity to challenge the strictures of the past and to find individual paths to spirituality under a God who seems more understanding and forgiving than the Deity depicted by close-minded theologians in the past.

Unlike many other Jewish American writers, Chaim Potok had no quarrel with his religion. Rather, he explored the conflict between Jewish values and culture and the values and culture of the secular American world. As a philosophical writer he was concerned with the question of the suffering not only of the Jewish people, but of all who are innocent. He addressed, by implication, the age-old question of theodicy: How can God's justice be validated in the face of the evil the Deity permits to exist?

Chaim Potok's father, Benjamin Max Potok, came to America from Poland after serving with a contingent of Poles in the Austrian army fighting the Russians in World War I. He worked as a jeweler and watchmaker in the then mostly Jewish section of the Bronx borough of New York City. He married Mollie Friedman, who was also a Jewish immigrant from Poland. The couple devoutly followed the faith of their ancestors. Benjamin was a Hassid, a member of the most traditional part of the Jewish religious community. Herman Harold Potok was born February 17, 1929, in the Bronx. As is the custom of Jews, he was given a Hebrew name, too. His was Chaim Tvzi. He grew up an observant Orthodox Jew like his parents. His childhood and early youth was spent immersed in a Jewish world.

Potok received a parochial primary education in Jewish schools, called yeshivas, in the Bronx. Besides required secular subjects, the curriculum centered on the beginning study of the Talmud, the 63 books of Jewish religious and ethical law based on the Hebrew Bible and the teachings of great rabbis.

Like millions of other people in America, Chaim's parents, small business people, struggled to get through the Great Depression from 1929 to 1939. Potok saw poverty, despair, and anti-Semitic violence. The gravest terror for young Chaim Potok and for his family came in the early years of World War II from the unfolding realization that European Jewry was systematically being murdered by the Germans under Hitler, and if the Allies did not stop them, they would come to America. Then the Potoks would go to the gas chambers of the death camps, too. Potok never forgot the Holocaust. That event, the greatest crime of the twentieth century, informs almost all of Potok's writing.

Chaim showed an early talent for drawing and painting, but in the Orthodox community the practice of art was considered a waste of time and perhaps even sinful, and so he found another channel for his creativity: writing. At the age of 14, Potok began to read the great Modernist writers such as James Joyce, William Faulkner, and Thomas Mann, despite the disapproval of family and community. He fell in love with the power of the creative imagination when it uses the written word to recreate the past, preserve the present, and express the moral dilemmas perennially facing humankind.

Potok attended the Talmudic Academy High School of Yeshiva University in Washington Heights, Manhattan, for his secondary education, which was Orthodox, not Hasidic, and therefore less extreme. Potok began to consider the possibility of a career as a writer of fiction in which he could interpret for general American readers the culture of his parents and his own generation of more secular American Jews.

Potok enrolled in Yeshiva University in Manhattan in 1946, a school with a rigorous program combining the liberal arts and sciences with intensive theological study. He began to write articles and short stories for the Yeshiva University yearbook and eventually became the editor. He received a bachelor of arts in English summa cum laude in 1950. At Yeshiva the strands of secular education and the love of literature, as well as further religious studies, entwined and structured Chaim Potok's intellectual and creative life. And at Yeshiva he made the critical decision to move his affiliation in the spectrum of American Jewish religious practice from Orthodox fundamentalism to the more centrist, more worldly, Conservative division.

After graduation Potok entered the Jewish Theological Seminary of America in New York City to study for the Conservative Jewish rabbinate. Once more he was an outstanding student, receiving several prizes including the Hebrew Literature Prize and the Bible Prize. In 1954 he was awarded the master of Hebrew literature degree and was ordained as a Conservative rabbi. Although as a clergyman Potok did not have to serve in the military during the Korean War, he was a patriotic American, and thus, he volunteered for army service as a combat chaplain. In Korea he worked with a forward area medical battalion—like a MASH unit without the comedy—attached to a combat engineer battalion. Potok served from the winding down of the conflict in 1955 to 1957. Attending to soldiers of all faiths, Potok was deeply moved by the shared humanity and the similar values and needs of all young soldiers. This experience would provide background and experience for Potok's novel

The Book of Lights (1981), in which two young friends begin their lives as rabbis by serving in Korea as chaplains. While still in Korea, Potok began four years of work on a novel about the beleaguered Asian country, but his war novel never found a publisher.

Leaving the army, Potok decided on a career in education instead of seeking a congregation to minister to. He accepted a position as a Jewish studies instructor at the University of Judaism in Los Angeles, and he taught there from 1957 to 1959. In 1958 Potok married Adena Sarah Mosevitzky, a psychiatric social worker. The young couple moved to Philadelphia in 1959 so that Potok could begin graduate work in philosophy at the University of Pennsylvania. Their daughter Rena was born in 1962.

Potok worked seven years on his first published novel. *The Chosen* (1967) is a story of the conflict between Hasidic and Orthodox Judaism in the 1940s played out in the relationship between a Hasidic youth, Danny, and an Orthodox boy, Reuven. It begins in rivalry and ends in deep friendship and mutual understanding. The book became a best-seller, was nominated for a National Book Award, and established the author as a significant American writer as well as interpreter of American Jewish culture.

The popularity of *The Chosen* was due in part to political events in the Western World. The Cold War had come upon us, troubling the Western democracies. One result was a revival of religion and religion-based writing. Many people, especially the young, sought ways of dealing with despair that included involvement in the drug culture, embracing oriental religions, or a return to traditional Western religions and their values.

In 1963 Potok had taken his family to Israel for a year. Part of the motivation for the sojourn was to make time to finish his doctoral dissertation. In moving to Israel Potok also wanted to distance himself from, and gain perspective on, the urban Jewish community he was writing about in *The Chosen*. Mainly, however, Israel beckoned to Potok because he desired, as did many intellectual American Jews of his generation, some first-hand experience with Zionism. For most Jews, Zionism represents not only the reconstitution of a Jewish national state for the first time since the second century C.E., but also a fulfillment of the biblical prophecy of the return to the Promised Land sadly longed for nearly two millennia. Many Jews and Christians today believe that this return to the homeland by the Jews precedes the coming of the Messiah, a God-anointed holy person who will relieve the Jewish people of their historic suffering and rebuild for the Jews in their own land the great Temple of Jerusalem. Christians, of course, believe that Jesus Christ is that Messiah who will return.

Then, in 1964, refreshed and profoundly moved by his sabbatical in Israel, Potok moved his family to the heart of the Hasidic world: Brooklyn. To earn his living Potok accepted a faculty appointment at the prestigious Teachers' Institute of the Jewish Theological Seminary of America where he had studied for his master's degree 10 years before. In Brooklyn Potok was near the most extremely religious Jewish community in the world, the Hasidim, Jews who experience Judaism with joy and emotion, with ecstatic singing and dancing, instead of with rabbinical, Talmudic learning.

In 1965 Adena and Chaim's second daughter, Naama, was born, and Potok was awarded the doctor of philosophy degree from the University of Pennsylvania upon the acceptance of his dissertation. He then went to work with the Jewish Publication Society of America, while making his final revisions of *The Chosen*, Potok's masterpiece, published in 1967. Potok had been made editor-in-chief of the Publication Society of America in 1966, and he remained in that capacity until 1974.

The Chosen received the Edward Lewis Wallant Prize and spent 39 weeks on the *New York Times* best-seller list. In 1968 the Potoks had their third and last child, their son, Akiva. Potok had already begun writing his second published novel, *The Promise* (1969), a sequel to *The Chosen*. It continues the story in the earlier novel of Danny and Reuven as they move into their respective careers and struggle to keep family antipathies from destroying their friendship. This novel received the Athenaeum Award.

Potok's third novel, *My Name Is Asher Lev* (1972), tells the story of an artist seeking an identity in an ultra-conservative society from which he is beginning to isolate himself. In 1973 the Potok family once again settled in Israel, living in Jerusalem, the capital of the country and the sacred city of the Jews. The Potoks lived there for four years and then returned to the United States to reside in Philadelphia where Potok once more took employment with the Jewish Publication Society of America, this time as special projects editor. *In the Beginning* was published in 1975. It is the story of a bright Jewish boy who, like Potok, is brought up in the Bronx and becomes a scholar of the Hebrew Bible. The novel questions how one is able to maintain his or her faith in the seemingly God-less world of the early twentieth century.

In 1978 Potok published his first nonfiction book, *Wanderings: Chaim Potok's History of the Jews*, in which he indicates how contemporary Jewish people can relate to the cultural package called Judaism from its origins onward. In 1981 *The Chosen* was made into a feature film. In 1983 Potok joined the Philosophy Department of the University of Pennsylvania as a visiting professor, teaching the philosophy of literature. He also was a visiting lecturer at nearby Bryn Mawr College in 1985 and at John Hopkins University in 1994, 1996, and 1997.

Potok's sixth novel, *Davita's Harp*, was published in 1985. For the first time the narrator is a female, Ilana Davita, who relates the story of her life from age 8 to 14 in the 1930s and 1940s. Davita's parents are committed communists, and they are disappointed because Davita is determined to think and decide for herself, looking for truth and the meaning of life in the Jewish and Christian traditions.

The Gift of Asher Lev appeared in 1990, winning the National Jewish Book Award. The novel is a sequel to *My Name Is Asher Lev* (1972). It continues Potok's concern with the perennial conflict between the artist and conventional society, antagonistic to the artist's product and way of life. Potok's eighth novel, *I Am the Clay*, followed in 1992. Now the author abandoned as his setting the Brooklyn Jewish community of the 1930s and 1940s for the country of Korea. It is a tale of the endurance of a brave Korean family with a will to survive as war ravages their country. Potok also wrote plays and children's books. Chaim Potok died in 2002 in his suburban home near Philadelphia.

PLOT DEVELOPMENT

A tightly controlled, carefully crafted novel, *The Chosen* is set in Williamsburg, a section of Brooklyn, where two Jewish groups, Hasidim and Orthodox worshipers, live in proximity but have little to do with each other because of religious differences. The time of the novel runs from early 1944 when World War II was raging, to 1948 with the founding of the State of Israel.

The Chosen is divided into three books. The first has 4 chapters; the second has 8 chapters; the third contains 6. The total number of chapters is 18, written in Hebrew with the character for the letter Ch'ai. The word is the same word as the word for "life." The letter/number is often worn around the neck as a good luck charm or to identify the wearer as Jewish. The Hebrew/ Jewish toast is "l'chayam." It means "to life." That there are 18 chapters in *The Chosen* is not a coincidence when the author is a student of Jewish holy and mystical books and whose Hebrew name is Chaim.

The Chosen opens dramatically. It is June 1944. The world is at war. In Brooklyn a softball game between two parochial school teams of Jewish boys turns into a holy war. The narrator, 15-year-old Reuven, attends an Orthodox parochial school. But he and his schoolmates don't wish to set themselves apart from the wider American community. Rather, they intend to go to college and either become rabbis, doctors, lawyers, or businessmen.

The opposing team is from an ultra-Orthodox Hasidic parochial school. The boys wear clothing and hairstyles that set them apart. For the most part they plan to go into small businesses where they can control their time so that work does not interfere with their religious obligations. The two groups of boys are at extreme variance over religious, political, and social matters.

As the game progresses in the schoolyard, the players become more and more aggressive. The ultra-Orthodox Hasidic boys, led by a boy named Danny, believe they are the righteous ones, and their merely Orthodox opponents, led by Reuven, are lost sinners. Reuven pitches to Danny, who purposely hits a vicious line drive at Reuven's head. The ball hits the upper rim of Reuven's eyeglasses and a piece of glass is driven into his left eye. In a hospital a skillful ophthalmologist removes the piece of glass in a delicate operation, and more than 100 pages later he pronounces the eye healed.

In the hospital Reuven Malter seethes with hatred for Danny Saunders. Having been informed of the injury to his son, Reuven's father, David Malter, rushes to his bedside. He is a secondary school teacher in an Orthodox yeshiva and a publishing scholar on the Talmud and other Jewish studies. The next day Mr. Malter informs Reuven that Danny's father, Reb (Rabbi) Saunders, has been calling to express his concern and sympathy for Reuven and to tell the Malters that Danny is very sorry for what has happened. Reuven, however, is doubtful of Danny's sincerity.

While Reuven is in his hospital bed, his eye heavily bandaged, D-Day arrives. The Americans, British, and Canadians land on the Normandy coast of German-occupied France. As great historical events are taking place, the injured Reuven is contemplating his future. His father wants him to be a mathematician as he is very good in math, but Reuven thinks he would rather become a rabbi.

When Danny appears at Reuven's bedside, the injured youth is amazed. Danny believes that Reuven hates him, and Reuven lies and says he doesn't. But he can't restrain himself and he curses Danny, hoping to make him feel guilty. Sorrowfully, Danny leaves, and it is Reuven who begins to experience guilt. The next day Danny comes back, and Reuven is more civil. To Danny's surprise the lonely patient is happy to see a boy his own age. Danny confesses that he wanted to kill Reuven, and he is trying to understand why he had felt that way. It was mainly because the communities that the boys had come from were so antagonistic to each other. Quickly the youths become friends. They are both "war" casualties: Reuven by the injury, and Danny, as it turns out, by the coldness of his father.

The youths begin to compare their education, and Reuven learns how hard Danny must study to satisfy his father, a Hasidic sect leader. Reuven's father is glad for the friendship. Unlike Reb Saunders, Mr. Malter is committed to bringing the differing Jewish communities together in the face of the common enemy: world fascism. Malter informs his son about European Judaism's tragic history. We later learn that Reb Saunders saved his community by leading them out of Russia after World War I and bringing them to America. Thus, they evaded Hitler's Holocaust.

As Reuven begins to attend Hasidic services with Danny and to eat with Danny's family, he learns to respect Reb Saunders and like the family. But Reuven will never be able to feel like anything but an outsider in the Hasidic community even though he comes to understand and respect it. To him it is a twilight world, something primitive, almost savage, and the raucous behavior in the synagogue appears carnivalesque.

Danny is continually queried and challenged by his father, who seems more intent on building up his son's reasoning and debating ability than on creating a loving relationship with him. Reuven enjoys watching their intellectual battles. Reb Saunders is hurt when he learns that his son reads English language books in the public library and is coming under the influence of Freud and Darwin, but he takes it as God's will.

Background to the maturation of the two young men and the growth of their friendship is the continuation of World War II. By the time of the Battle of the Bulge in January 1945, the high school students are seeing little of each other, enmeshed as they are in their serious studies and college preparation. The war in Europe ends, and news of the Holocaust comes through to shock the minds and the hearts of the people of the world. A flu epidemic has stricken Danny, Reuven, and the weakened Mr. Malter, who has been hurled into a deep depression by the revelation of the horrors of the German death camps. Then Mr. Malter suffers a heart attack. Reuven cannot be left with a housekeeper who comes in to make meals, so Reb Saunders invites him to live with his family and share a room with Danny until his father recovers. Reuven is generously accepted as a member of the family, and the two friends are united for a few summer months.

Whenever Reuven visits his father in the hospital, the main topic of discussion is the destruction of European Jewry and the indifference of Western democracies, like Britain and the United States, to their fate. In the autumn of 1945 Mr. Malter has recovered. The war has ended with the dropping of atomic bombs on Japan. The young men, as planned, enroll in the same school, Hirsch College, a combination seminary and secular institution in Brooklyn. Danny studies psychology as well as Talmud. He is able to read Freud in the original German. More and more, he feels desperately trapped by his father's dream that he will succeed him as leader of the sect.

Meanwhile, a great conflict tears Hirsch College apart. Teachers and students who are ultra-Orthodox believe that only the Messiah can re-establish

the ancient State of Israel. The Zionist students and faculty support the establishment of the new state. Many questions arise and are debated such as: Can
an American Jew have allegiance to the United States and to Israel simultaneously? What would a Jewish person do if America and Israel went to war with
each other?

Reuven, like his father, is a Zionist. Danny does not join either side
although his heart is with the Zionists. But Danny is not allowed to continue
communication with his friend. Reb Saunders has forbidden it. The Malters'
Zionism was the last straw. The friendship is shattered. But the wise and compassionate Mr. Malter understands and explains to his son that the fanaticism
of people like Reb Saunders has kept Judaism alive through 2,000 years of
persecution.

For months the two college students are in constant proximity but not
speaking to each other. Reuven feels only hatred for Reb Saunders, who has
deprived the young men of their close friendship. In 1947 the United Nations
voted for partition of Palestine into two states, one Jewish and one Arab.
Reuven and his father are ecstatic, but in Hirsch College Zionist and anti-
Zionist students are close to blows. Mr. Malter has his second heart attack
and is rushed to the hospital. At school Danny brushes Reuven's hand with
his as a gesture of understanding and sympathy, and thus the suffering of
Mr. Malter restores the friendship. In May of 1948, after a final enabling vote
by the United Nations, Israel proclaimed its independence and began a life
and death struggle with the armies of all of its Arab neighbors. With that desperate struggle going on, the anti-Zionist sentiment in the college disappears.

In September, Mr. Malter is well enough to return to his teaching and his
scholarship. Anti-Zionism also dies out in the ultra-Orthodox community,
and in the spring of 1949 Danny is allowed once more to talk to his friend.
They had endured a painful silence for two years. Reb Saunders has aged
considerably. His defeat in the battle for the soul of the Jewish people has
had a bad effect on his spirit and his health. In their last year at college, the
young men affirm their commitments to their respective professions: the rabbinate for Reuven and clinical psychology for Danny after a Ph.D. Danny's
younger brother is now destined to become the "tzaddik," the leader of his
father's sect.

Reuven is deeply distressed by Danny's problems of family and conscience.
He wants to help Danny, and he has truly learned a lesson that his father has
taught him, that it is not easy to be a true friend. In the climactic scene of
the novel Reb Saunders recognizes and accepts that Danny will be different
from him, and he explains to Reuven that he only wants Danny to have a
compassionate soul, for a great soul is more important than knowledge. The

rabbi begs forgiveness from Reuven for hating his father's Zionism, and from Danny for not being a kinder, gentler, more communicating father. The scene ends in tears of love and understanding in the eyes of the young men, and the departure of a weary old man, loved and respected, too. Danny and Reuven graduate summa cum laude, eager and hungry for their futures. In the end Reb Saunders accepts Danny's decision to go to Columbia University to study psychology, and he gives his son his blessings. When we last see Danny he has shaved off his beard and cut his earlocks.

CHARACTER DEVELOPMENT

Four characters dominate *The Chosen:* Danny Saunders; his father, Rabbi Saunders; Reuven Malter; and his father, David Malter. Potok writes as if he were composing an opera. He presents duets: Danny and Reuven, Reuven and his father, Danny and his father. There are trios: Danny, Reuven, and Mr. Malter; Danny, Reuven, and Rabbi Saunders. But there are no quartets. The fathers respect each other from a distance, although for a while Reb Saunders hates Mr. Malter for his Zionist activism. Potok keeps them separate because their respective political positions are irreconcilable, and bringing them together would have been so explosive as to shift the focus of the novel from the younger generation to the older.

Danny Saunders is the central character of the novel. He is a child prodigy, a genius whose father sees himself reincarnated in the brilliant son he is sure will inherit the leadership of the Hasidic sect they belong to. The Hasidic congregation deifies him almost as much as his father; he is their crown prince. It is Danny who experiences the greatest change and suffers the most. He leads a double life, secretly assimilating Western knowledge while appearing to conform to his father's image of a Hasidic leader in training. It is Danny who must confront and win out over an authoritarian, if well-meaning, father. He must break with a smothering, stultifying tradition to learn to serve humankind through psychology, a way not approved by the fundamentalist religious sect he was born into.

Freud become a passion and an obsession with Danny, because the one thing Danny most needs to understand is why his father almost never talks to him except when they are studying the Talmud together. Ironically, Danny is required to become a rabbi even though he does not want to be one, while Reuven wants to become a rabbi even though he does not have to.

Reuven is the point-of-view character, observing and narrating the milieu of his childhood and youth. He must find his Jewish identity for himself, because his wise and sensitive father is not didactic. Potok exposes his narrator to the Hasidic world precisely so that the youth can sample it, reject it as impractical and confining, and yet understand and appreciate it. We like him more than Danny. He is more human. Geniuses are hard for us to be around. When Reuven is an ordained rabbi, he will bring assimilated Jews back to the synagogue and educate their children in Jewish law and Jewish customs. Thus, he will help to create a vitalized American Jewish community that in a sense will replace what was lost in Europe.

Reuven is a loyal friend to Danny. He is a good listener, and his counsel is generally wise and understanding. Reuven's great efforts as a student show the determination and perseverance that insures success. He is logical and scientific. Through his hospital experience and the suffering and fear his wounded eye gave him, he has developed compassion for others.

Middle-aged, thin, pale, tired, and unwell, David Malter is an idealized teacher of Jewish studies, dedicated to his Talmudic scholarship, yet a humanitarian. He encourages rational explanations in textual studies. Unlike Rabbi Saunders and the Hasids, he believes that God is approachable to individual people. Mr. Malter believes that Western secular culture is not an enemy to Jewish life; rather, it has much good to offer if employed judiciously. He advocates intellectual inquiry. Holy texts are to be explicated rationally. Jewish law must be interpreted in such a way as to blend tradition with modern ideas, scientific fact, and human needs.

Mr. Malter deeply loves his son, who is clearly the most important person in his life. He is a good single parent, who never tries to relive his life or clone himself through his bright son. Mr. Malter is Potok's projection of what a good parent should be. Mr. Malter learns a very powerful, if painful, lesson in middle age: no minority is impervious to the machinations of the outside world. A people, no matter how much they love and worship God, no matter how moral and ethical their daily lives, should not be passive in the matter of their own survival. Only at their peril do they live with heads in the sand or in the clouds. Although essentially a contemplative person, Mr. Malter is stirred to action by the awful knowledge of the Holocaust, and he throws himself into a passionate cause for the first time in his life: the realization of Zionism in the establishment of the Jewish State of Israel.

Rabbi Saunders is perhaps the most interesting and complex of the main characters in *The Chosen*. He is the charismatic hereditary leader of a religious sect that sees him as infallible and comes close to worshipping him. He is self-righteous. He scorns all seemingly frivolous discourse. He is unfeeling and cold toward his son, mistaking training in memorization and recall for ethical and moral instruction. He rages and domineers. Yet he is impotent outside his tiny principality. He cannot even keep his son from being influenced by the outside world.

However, in the end the reader has sympathy and even admiration for Reb Saunders. He did what he thought best for his son and his dependent community. It is not an easy task to serve a community that expects its leader to be all-knowing and all-wise. Saunders showed compassion for Reuven when the young man was injured and when his father was ill. He suffered for what the world did to the Jewish people, and that suffering was not made easier because he believed it was God's will. Almost blasphemously, he asks the Master of the Universe how He could permit the Holocaust to happen.

THEMES

The great external theme of *The Chosen* is the Holocaust and its aftermath, its impact on Jewish America, and its significance as a prelude to the founding of the State of Israel. Much of the last third of the story reflects the struggle over Zionism in the Jewish community, as well as the world-wide efforts of Zionists to establish the new state. The conflict over loyalties engaged in by American Jews is manifested in the novel by the dispute between David Malter and Reb Saunders. It is presaged by the fateful softball game at the story's beginning.

A second theme is that of the manifestations of the American Dream. *The Chosen* affirms a uniquely American kind of optimism and idealism. Danny and Reuven are children of immigrants, but they are well educated. The young men take for granted that they have occupational choices, and that they will have bright futures as long as they are willing to work as hard in the world as they have done in school. They assume that there will be equal opportunity for them. If they think at all about encountering discrimination, they are confident they can overcome it. Lastly, they are unaware of the uniqueness of American opportunity for Jews and other minorities because they don't compare their lives with those young Jews who had the misfortune of living in Europe.

A third and perhaps most significant theme in *The Chosen* is that of father–son conflict, in this case Danny and Reb Saunders. The struggle is nonviolent and mainly fought out on the psychological battlefield. Saunders expects his brilliant son to succeed him as leader of his Hasidic sect. He tries to restrict Danny's reading to religious books. He fears his son will fall victim to acculturation in the gentile world. He is intimidating and controlling by the implied threat of disapproval. Furthermore, the power of the community and the weight of ancient tradition serve his will.

The attempted mind control makes Danny physically ill and depressed, but Danny is already "infected" by Western knowledge and culture as well as American secularism. Danny is fighting for freedom of thought, intellectual inquiry, and action. Of course, the son wins in the end. It is the way of the world. The father–son conflict in *The Chosen* is a microcosm of intrafamily struggles between generations of Jewish children rejecting the values and strictures of their parents, only in many cases to return to at least some of them when they themselves are parents.

NARRATIVE STYLE

The main subject of the book is the developing friendship between two young men from opposing communities, and the way their friendship overcomes the impediments placed in their path primarily by members of the older generation. One of the suspenseful plot lines of the novel is woven around the possibility that Reuven could lose sight in one eye. Another is the tension between Danny and his father and whether Danny can abdicate leadership and break free from his father's dream.

Potok has excellent descriptive powers. His portrait of the closed world of Brooklyn Hasidism is fascinating to the reader. The accuracy, detail, and richness of his presentation of the seemingly exotic community and their environs is like a travelogue to a foreign place inhabited by a very different people. This is not only the experience of the reader; it is Reuven's, the point-of-view character and narrator.

One might also compare aspects of the novel to a documentary film depicting a society radically different from mainstream America. A camera eye seems to roam the streets and enter into homes, schools, and synagogues with Reuven. The descriptions of the feasting of the Hasidim point out the importance of food in that culture. This documentary quality is emphasized by the frequent interjections of background "essays" on the historical evolution and the customs of the Hasidic community. However, this can be somewhat off-putting as it delays the narrative flow. The serious reader must slow down and absorb the lessons to be learned from *The Chosen*.

Potok's decision to use a first-person narrative for the telling of the story works particularly well. Reuven is appealing as a personality, and he is easy to identify with for young people. This technique is compatible with Potok's role as a teaching writer.

Special attention should be paid to Potok's brilliant use of eye imagery in the novel. Eye, eyes, and eyeglasses symbolize seeing, opening up of vision, insight, and recognition. At the beginning of the novel, as the ballgame begins, Reuven keeps pushing up his glasses on the bridge of his nose so that they won't fall off during action. This description establishes Reuven as a serious student, a reader, but also it foreshadows the accident to his eye that will happen shortly when it is struck by a piece of eyeglass. Glasses are both a way of seeing better and a barrier to the world. The glasses are broken. The sliver that enters his eye symbolically opens his eyes to the Hasidic world of his future friend. Also, the suffering that Reuven endures because of his eye injury makes him more understanding of the suffering of others, starting with fellow patients in the eye ward of the hospital.

When Danny is learning about earlier Jewish history, he recognizes that people are complicated because they are blind to themselves; that is, they lack insight. As Danny comes to "see" more and more of the outside world, his eyes blink. Finally, as the young men have matured to their full height and have begun to grow facial hair, Danny begins to wear glasses too. Discovering the secular world that he finds so fascinating requires the assistance of another set of eyes, so to speak. But eyes have other functions besides seeing. When Danny is forbidden to speak to Reuven, they communicate with their eyes. The final eye reference in the novel is on the last page, when Danny's eyes glow as he realizes that he soon will be studying at Columbia University where vast cultural vistas are waiting to be seen.

HISTORICAL BACKGROUND

The time of *The Chosen*, as stated previously, is the period between the last days of World War II and the establishment of the State of Israel. The central historical event in the novel is the Holocaust. For Reb Saunders the Holocaust and international anti-Semitism is God's will. He sees only the truth he wishes to see: the world always slaughters Jews. For Mr. Malter and Reuven, Reb Saunders's answer is unsatisfactory, and his genuine tears of sorrow are of little use. They believe that Jews must now make their own destiny. The answer for the Malters is the sovereign State of Israel, the land of refuge for the survivors of the German slaughter and for future generations if persecuted where they sojourn.

Reuven makes the mistake of broaching the idea of Israel to the Saunders family, and the Rabbi is infuriated. For Reb Saunders, non-Hasidic Jews are really gentiles. Zionists would only contaminate the Holy Land. It is for the Messiah to re-establish the state of Israel.

Mr. Malter fights for the establishment of a Jewish state despite the opposition of the British authorities in the Palestine Mandate and the Arab population. His lesson for Reuven is that a person must make his life a meaningful one. The meaning of one's life is ultimately more important than the life itself. David Malter belatedly finds meaning for his life in Zionism. The Holocaust can only have meaning in the concept of a universe created and watched over by God if it brings about the return of the Jewish people to their ancient land. Reuven, however, will find meaning in the life of a rabbi, reorienting and reeducating secularized American Jewry.

Potok used history as a structural device to support his plot. The reader, knowledgeable about the outcome of World War II and the post-war struggle of the survivors of the Holocaust to establish the State of Israel, nevertheless shares the suspense seemingly felt by the fictional characters living in the momentous years from 1944 through 1948.

SUGGESTED READINGS

Primary Source

Potok, Chaim. *The Chosen*. New York: Simon and Schuster, 1967.

Secondary Sources

Abramson, Edward A. *Chaim Potok*. Boston: Twayne, 1986.
Sternlicht, Sanford. *Chaim Potok: A Critical Companion*. Westport, Conn.: Greenwood, 2000.

9

Philip Roth
Portnoy's Complaint
(1969)

Unlike Bernard Malamud in *The Assistant,* Philip Roth in *Portnoy's Complaint* does not use Jewishness as a platform for universalizing human experience. He uses it to humorously and satirically particularize the possible Oedipal conflicts a Jewish American male might experience, or try to avoid, growing up in mid-twentieth-century America. *Portnoy's Complaint* is a dark comedy of psychological suffering. It is also an act of provocation on the part of a talented and ambitious author, but it is not an act of Jewish self-hatred. It should be read for what it is: a brilliant work of satirical fiction.

Portnoy's Complaint seemed a radical novel in the 1960s. Today, its treatment of sexuality and use of scatology are not shocking. Instead, the novel is widely considered a masterpiece in the satiric modernist tradition, like James Joyce's bildungsroman *Portrait of the Artist as a Young Man.*

BIOGRAPHICAL CONTEXT

Philip Milton Roth was born on March 19, 1933, in Newark, New Jersey, where his father, Herman Roth, the American-born son of Jewish immigrants from Poland, owned a shoe store. His mother, Bess Finkel Roth, was also the child of immigrants. The shoe store failed in the Depression, and Herman became a salesman for the Metropolitan Life Insurance Company. After many years of toil in the streets as a door-to-door salesman, he was promoted to an executive position, managing an office with many employees. His career was unusual, as few Jews had ever risen to executive rank in the company.

From 1946 to 1950 Philip Roth attended Weequahic High School in a largely Jewish section of Newark. From 1950 to 1951 he attended Newark College of Rutgers University, and then he transferred to Bucknell University, where he published his first story in a campus literary magazine. A second story was published in the prestigious *Chicago Review*. Roth received a B.A. in English from Bucknell in 1954. He then went on to take an M.A. in English at the University of Chicago in 1955. To fulfill his military obligation during a time of the draft, he joined the army but was quickly given a medical discharge after suffering a back injury in basic training.

Returning to the University of Chicago, Roth entered the Ph.D. program in 1956 and became an instructor in English. At this time he met Saul Bellow, who would become his mentor and life-long friend. While at the University of Chicago, one of Roth's stories was chosen for *The Best Short Stories of 1956*. Roth then knew he would have a career in writing. He left the university in 1958 for full-time writing. The next year he received a Guggenheim Fellowship, and with the publication of *Good-Bye Columbus* (1959), a collection of short stories, Roth established his reputation as an important young American writer when he received the National Book Award.

In 1962 Roth was a writer-in-residence at Princeton University. He subsequently taught at Hunter College, the University of Iowa, and the University of Pennsylvania. Roth's first novel, *Letting Go*, a somewhat affected story of young Jewish intellectuals in Chicago and New York, was published in 1962. From 1962 to 1967 Roth, suffering from writer's block, underwent psychoanalysis in New York City. His next novel, *When She Was Good* (1967), is set in the Midwest and features an imperious Protestant housewife. Although Roth's first two novels were not impressive, the third, *Portnoy's Complaint* (1969), benefiting from his psychoanalysis, was a sensational success.

Our Gang (1971) was Roth's first political novel. It savages "President Trick E. Dixon" through over-the-top satire. *The Breast* (1972) owes much to Franz Kafka. It tells the story of a Jewish academic named David Kapesh who wakes up to find that he has metamorphosed into a huge female breast. *The Great American Novel* (1973) is a comic baseball allegory on the destructiveness of competitive life in America. *My Life as a Man* (1974) has a writer named Peter Tarnopol writing about a writer named Nathan Zuckerman. Zuckerman will return as the protagonist in several subsequent Roth novels. *The Professor of Desire* (1977) brings David Kapesh back to endure angst-filled relationships with women.

The Ghost Writer (1979) is the first full Nathan Zuckerman novel, in which Zuckerman has an affair with a woman whom he imagines to be Anne Frank. Zuckerman lives on in *Zuckerman Unbound* (1981), where he faces the peril of publishing a controversial novel like *Portnoy's Complaint*, and in *The Anatomy Lesson* (1983) where Zuckerman, now bald and broken in health, faces a career crisis. These three novels and the story "The Prague Orgy" were combined to form *Zuckerman Bound: A Trilogy and Epilogue* (1985).

The Counterlife (1986) has Zuckerman and his brother deal with their impotencies in a radically sacrilegious story in which Jewish life in Israel is the "counterlife" to that in the Diaspora. Roth suffered a deep depression in late 1987 precipitated by prescription painkillers taken after a difficult and painful knee operation. He then had open-heart surgery in 1989.

Deception: A Novel (1990) is about a middle-aged American whose name is Philip, and who is having an affair with a married English woman. In 1991 Roth received the National Arts Club's Medal of Honor for Literature for the body of this work. *Operation Shylock: A Confession* (1993) is an amazing experimental novel in which a novelist, whose name is Philip Roth, is having a breakdown while an imposter is using his name. *Sabbath's Theater* (1995) is a comedic novel featuring an old, disgraced, suicidal puppeteer. It won a second National Book Award for Roth. *American Pastoral* (1997) was awarded the Pulitzer Prize for fiction. In it Nathan Zuckerman relates the life of a boyhood sports idol whose adult life is destroyed when the daughter he loves becomes a terrorist. In this same year Roth underwent surgery for prostate cancer.

I Married a Communist (1998) is about a radio actor blacklisted in the McCarthy era, and who is a Zuckerman hero, but whose disgruntled wife publishes a book depicting her husband's slavish adherence to the Communist Party. *The Human Stain* (2000) is the poignant and tragic story of an academic with an ethnicity secret who is falsely accused of racism. *The Dying Animal* (2001) brings back David Kapesh and deals with the pervasiveness of the erotic impulse as well as love and death. *The Plot Against America* (2004) has Roth fantasying about the possible fate of Jews if American Nazis under Charles Lindberg had attempted to take over the United States in the 1940s. *Everyman* (2006) chronicles an anonymous New York man's life through regrets, aging, and illness, to his death.

Roth married Margaret Martinson Williams, a divorced woman with a child, in 1959. It was not a happy marriage. They were legally separated in 1963, but Margaret refused to allow a divorce, and so they were legally married until she died in a car crash in 1968. Roth did not marry a second time until 1990, when he married the British actress Claire Bloom, with whom he had been living for many years. Their marriage ended in 1995. Roth has lived in Chicago, Rome, London, and New York City. He currently resides in rural Connecticut.

PLOT DEVELOPMENT

Portnoy's Complaint is the sexual autobiography of a 33-year old lawyer, who compulsively attempts to free himself from the strict confines of his Jewish upbringing and the torment of a smother-loving mother and a perpetually constipated father. His guilt-ridden escape comes through sexual activity: first masturbation and then sexual conquest. The novel is a long monologue delivered by Alexander Portnoy, New York City's Assistant Commissioner of Human Opportunity, to his Freudian psychoanalyst, the Jewish, German-trained, Dr. Spielvogel.

The format of the psychoanalysis session allowed Roth to speak fully and frankly about sex, because psychoanalysis often focuses on the patients' sex-related problems.

The novel is divided into six sections. The first two, "The Most Unforgettable Character I've Ever Met" and "Whacking Off," depict Alexander's childhood and adolescence growing up in Newark, New Jersey, during the Depression and the World War II years. He comments on the events of his early life by reflecting on his strained relationship with his domineering and controlling mother and his stressed father. Alexander attempts to escape from the action-drama of his suffocating home life through rebellious words and actions.

"Jewish Blues," section three, focuses on intergenerational conflicts in which the maturing and intelligent Alexander pits his humanistic and secular values against those of his parents and the conservative Jewish community that want to inculcate "Jewishness" into the fractious youth. The longest section of the novel, "Cunt Crazy," focuses humorously on Alexander's adolescent sexual fantasies, including the belief that his father had an affair with a gentile cashier in his office. In this section, the fourth, Alexander introduces Mary Jane Reed, aka The Monkey, a poorly educated but very beautiful fashion model who is the source of his sexual liberation as well as his great grief, for she is determined to marry him, and he is not only unprepared for marriage, but can't see himself tied to someone who is almost illiterate. Alexander's calling Mary Jane The Monkey is a reference to her sexual acrobatics, but also a way in which he dehumanizes a woman to avoid commitment.

Alexander also states his belief that Jewish mothers symbolically castrate their sons and sometimes drive them to homosexuality or suicide. He is determined to resist these fates by indulging in an unrelenting pursuit of sex with gentile women whom he can't marry, because he has been programmed by his parents and his culture to marry only in the faith.

"The Most Prevalent Form of Degradation in Erotic Life," the fifth section, flashes back to Alexander's college romance with a gentile girl from the Midwest whose hometown seems like a foreign country to him; and a later love, a woman from an upper-class New England background. Both women are left deeply disappointed as Alexander aggressively soldiers on in the love wars. It seems he has been trying to discover America by sleeping with women of different classes and from different regions. Hello, Columbus.

Finally, in the last section, "In Exile," Alexander flees to Israel and is thrilled by experiencing a country where everyone from the trash collector to the university professor is Jewish. But his encounters with female sabres (Jews born in Israel) are disastrous. They are strong, tough, intelligent women, with little appreciation for nervous, diasporic Jewish men with hang-ups. For the first time, Alexander is impotent. Returning home for therapy, he ends up howling in Dr. Spielvogel's office. When he stops, the psychoanalyst informs him that now they can begin their work.

CHARACTER DEVELOPMENT

Except for Mary Jane Reed, the main characters of *Portnoy's Complaint* are to a certain degree stereotypical. Collectively, they are secularized Jews without Judaism. Ultimately they seem pathetic. Also pathetic are Alexander's many shiksa conquests.

Roth does not love his protagonist. Alexander is a Jewish momma's boy: intelligent, oral, neurotic, sometimes hysterical, Oedipally fixated, and thus always chasing the golden shiksa in order to avoid psychological incest (Mom). He is a complainer, a nudge, whose political liberalism masks his selfishness and predacious nature. He uses women like Kleenex.

Through analysis, the talking cure, Alexander is hoping to find relief from his guilt, angst, and self-disgust for not being able to live up to his parents' impossible expectations. His suffering is genuine. Moreover, the conscience in Alexander's Jewish head prevents him from truly enjoying the hedonistic pleasures he lives for, while his rational intelligence punishes him mercilessly by exposing the hypocrisy and futility of his life.

Sophie Portnoy is the Jewish mother from hell: nagging, controlling, bullying, boastful, insensitive, ignorant, sarcastic, xenophobic, bigoted, materialistic, and pathologically smother-loving. She loves but does not respect her husband. Roth's treatment of the Jewish mother is sometimes sympathetic, but more often is close to matricidal. Through Sophie, Roth effectively killed off the Jewish mother in American fiction.

Yet Roth understands the underlying pain and anxiety of a Jewish mother in the 1940s. She is fearful of all kinds of things that could harm her beloved son, her "lover" as she calls him. She does not want him to flush the toilet, because she wants to see and evaluate what is in the bowl. Maybe he ate bad food like French fries and ketchup. Sophie's fear of the outside anti-Semitic world is designed to protect but, in fact, inflicts much psychic violence. It is Sophie who is "The Most Unforgettable Character I've Ever Met."

Jack Portnoy is the prototypical Jewish father: hard working, honest, emotional, somewhat vulgar, paranoid, worrisome, spiritually eviscerated, and uxorious. He is unable to mediate between his super-powerful wife and his pride-and-joy son. Perhaps this is a main source of his chronic constipation. (Between Alexander's masturbation and Jack's constipation, one would have to sign up for toilet time in the Portnoy household.)

Hannah, the Jewish sister/daughter in the traditional two-child Jewish American family, is bright, homely, loyal, ameliorating, ignorant about the pleasures of sex, and possibly doomed to become her mother. After all, the Jewish mothers have to come from somewhere. But the sister is spared maternal aggression because she is a female and thus not worth the strangulation visited on her poor brother. Hannah marries a normal, ordinary Jewish man, and they have children.

The Monkey is an uneducated, good-hearted, working-class, sweet-talking, Southern blonde: a lascivious, long-legged, provocatively-dressing model. Mary Jane is loyal. Her loyalty to Alexander and even to her millionaire neurotic first husband, whom she married at age 18, is a quality Alexander can't understand. She has come to her liberated sexuality despite a horrific childhood. She invokes the reader's sympathy because, sadly, she seems only able to establish human relations through sex, because she wrongly believes that is all she has to give. Her willingness to accommodate Alexander's sexual fantasies extends even to the point of agreeing to an orgy with an Italian prostitute. Mary Jane Reed deserved better than Alexander Portnoy.

THEMES

A main theme of *Portnoy's Complaint*, the tension between license and restraint, was a perfect one for the late 1960s and early 1970s. Yet there is always a struggle between the hunger for personal liberty and the forces of inhibition. In the case (psychiatric) of Alexander Portnoy, the forces of inhibition come from his parents and the fearful, controlling, fading old-world culture they represent. Alexander unconsciously hopes to escape through what proves to be the impossible: slipping loose from his Jewish identity. This is a frequent theme in Jewish American writers of the Bellow, Malamud, and

Roth generations. Alexander hopes that the conquest of gentile women, as well as his success in New York City government, will shorten the length of his nose, straighten his curly hair, and let him pass as a gentile. The goal of passing, of abandoning the values of his family and his tribe, is another theme, and it is perhaps the source of the guilt that has caused Alexander's neurosis.

Another major theme in *Portnoy's Complaint* is Momism, a term coined by the sociologist Philip Wylie and current in the 1950s and 1960s. It stands for an excessive attachment toward one's mother, who over protects and over controls; her unconscious goal is to establish life-long dependency. Sophie Portnoy is the most obvious literary example of this exaggerated and unfair portrait of motherhood: Irish, Italian, Chinese, or Jewish. However, in *Portnoy's Complaint* Momism is very funny.

NARRATIVE STYLE

Portnoy's Complaint is a stream-of-humor novel. In that sense it is much like the rapid fire spiel of an old-time Yiddish comedian, not adverse to throwing in a little shmutz (dirt) while playing the schlemiel (jerk) and laying one joke on top of another until the audience is convulsed. In fact, Alexander states that he is living his life in a Jewish joke. The novel is structured as a diatribe in the form of a confession from an analysand. Alexander, the impatient patient, reveals a series of events that produced the guilt that plagues his existence.

Roth juxtaposes Alexander's narrative of actual events with a parallel set of fantasies. Indeed, the reader sometimes is baffled as to what is real and what is fantasy. After all, Alexander is not a well man. He is prone, for example, to vast linguistic exaggeration throughout the text. Roth exaggerates to perfection. This is a significant part of Roth's comic art and achievement. For example: Sophie describes the success of a friend's "son the doctor" in hilarious cascades of impossible overstatements such as when she declares that the doctor is the biggest brain surgeon in the Western hemisphere. He has not one, but six split-level ranch houses. Best of all, he takes his entire family on a tour through Europe: all 7,000 countries. Beat that Alexander, Jewish son, if you can.

Roth's use of metaphor is often worthy of poetry, as when Alexander compares his parents' ability to produce guilt in him to rendering fat from a chicken. Or when he compares his disappearing testicle—fleeing from the scrotum into the body cavity to escape the knife Sophie frequently flourishes—as a shipwrecked sailor being dragged from the sea into a lifeboat. *Portnoy's Complaint* is a virtuoso performance of language art and a comedy of Eros. Bouncy prose rhythms produce a fast moving text. The reader is on a linguistic roller coaster. High volume exchanges punctuate the text as characters scream at each other like newspaper headlines in rival tabloids.

HISTORICAL CONTEXT

The 1960s in the United States was an era of new freedoms. There was a sexual revolution brought about in part by the birth control pill that gave women a control over pregnancy that they never before had. The 1960s really "let go" and "let it all hang out." *Playboy Magazine* was the most successful new periodical of the time. In 1969 *Portnoy's Complaint* found a premier place in the counterculture, the New Left that hated the materialists, vulgarians, hypocrites, and hypocritical government leaders who had dominated the nation, dragging it into the Vietnam War.

Portnoy's crazed lust appears as a sign of liberation, and that liberation was deemed healthy. Roth placed himself among the leaders of the avant-garde cultural parade under the banners of sexual and rhetorical freedom. Masturbation, that dark secret, was now discussible in fiction. Orgies could be described without censorship or condemnation. Urban young were delighted with *Portnoy's Complaint*. It was antidote to the fearful claustrophobia of their anxious parents and grandparents. The old puritanical society was buried for at least two decades: that is, until the arrival of AIDS.

SUGGESTED READINGS

Primary Sources

Roth, Philip. *The Facts: A Novelist's Autobiography*. New York: Farrar, Straus & Giroux, 1988.
———. *Patrimony: A True Story*. New York: Simon and Schuster, 1991.
———. *Portnoy's Complaint*. New York: Random House, 1969.

Secondary Sources

Cooper, Alan. *Philip Roth and the Jews*. Albany: State University of New York Press, 1996.
Halio, Jay L. *Philip Roth Revisited*. New York: Twayne, 1992.
Jones, Judith Peterson, and A. Guinevera. *Philip Roth*. New York: Frederick Ungar, 1981.
McDaniel, John N. *The Fiction of Philip Roth*. Haddonfield, N.J.: Haddonfield House, 1974.
Rodgers, Bernard F., Jr. *Philip Roth*. Boston: Twayne, 1978.

10

Cynthia Ozick
The Messiah of Stockholm
(1987)

The Messiah of Stockholm is a powerful story about the archetypal quest for a father even when there is really no hope of finding him. That poignant and passionate desire is linked to the perennial hope of the Jewish people for the coming of the Messiah. It is also about a human being's overriding need for an identity.

BIOGRAPHICAL CONTEXT

Cynthia Ozick is a writer of remarkable intelligence and learning. She is a philosopher, satirist, and critic. Her imagination stretches from naturalistic reproduction to intriguing fantasy. Ozick was born in New York City on April 17, 1928, the daughter of a pharmacist, William Ozick, and Celia Regelson Ozick. Cynthia was only one generation removed from the vibrant culture of the Lower East Side of Manhattan immigrant Jewish community. Growing up in the Bronx, she was an avid reader among a generation of Jewish youth who fell in love with secular literature. She attended Hunter College High School, and she received her B.A. cum laude in English in 1949 from New York University, where she was Phi Beta Kappa. She taught from 1949 to 1951 at Ohio State University, earning her M.A. there in 1950. In 1952 Ozick married an attorney, Bernard Hallote. A daughter was born in 1965. Ozick returned to New York and to New York University in 1964 to teach English. Shortly afterward she became a full-time writer.

Ozick's first novel, *Trust* (1965), is a long work depicting a vivid panorama of the social and political life of the wealthy in New York and Europe from the 1930s to the 1960s. It impressed critics, but was deemed too derivative of Henry James, the subject of Ozick's master's thesis. Shying away from the novel form, Ozick published her first collection of short stories, *The Pagan Rabbi and Other Stories*, in 1971. The book was received with rapture by the critics because it announced a fresh, brilliant voice in Jewish American fiction. A second collection, *Bloodshed and Three Novellas* (1976), includes shockingly ironic stories of the Holocaust and its effect on Jewry. The stories show the influence of Nobel Prize-winning Isaac Bashevis Singer's spirituality on Ozick's development. Another successful story collection, *Levitation: Five Fictions* (1982), contains tales concerning the need Jews have to study and know their past in order to explain their collective survival. The collection also deals with Jewish writers trying to gain access to the exclusive celebrity world of Jewish American fiction.

Ozick's second novel, *The Cannibal Galaxy* (1983), offers a dispassionate analysis of Jewish education—the afternoon Hebrew school and the Sunday school—in America, as two cultures clash: secular Western culture and Rabbinic Judaism. *The Messiah of Stockholm* (1987) affirmed Ozick's stature as an important American writer.

The Shawl (1989) contains two stories, "The Shawl" and "Rosa," linked by imagery and events. The former is particularly significant because, for the first time, Ozick fully engages the hell that was the Holocaust through the experience of a victim.

In 1994 in New York, Sidney Lumet directed Ozick's play *Blue Light*, based on "The Shawl" and "Rosa." It is a frighteningly provocative drama set in Auschwitz during the time of the gas chambers and 30 years later. *The Puttermesser Papers* (1997) depicts the life and times of an intellectual woman more interested in reading than romance. The message is that life is for living, and even a butter knife (*Puttermesser*) could cut through life to its essence. *Heir to the Glimmering World* (2004; published in the United Kingdom as *The Bear Boy* in 2006) is the engrossing story of an intellectual, but neurotic, German Jewish refugee family in New York City in 1935 as seen through the eyes of an 18-year-old orphaned girl who is the nanny.

Cynthia Ozick has published several highly regarded volumes of social and literary criticism. She has received honorary doctorates from Yeshiva University and Hebrew Union College. Her other awards include the Jewish Book Council Epstein Award (1972 and 1977), the Lamport Prize (1980), a Guggenheim Fellowship (1982), and the American Academy of Arts and Letters Strauss Living Award (1983).

PLOT DEVELOPMENT

The Messiah of Stockholm is the story of Lars Andemening, a 42-year-old unkempt man living in a small apartment in Stockholm where he works as a reviewer for a newspaper. He has married twice. His first wife divorced him because he seemed to have "an irregular spirit." He fought with his second wife, and she ran off to America with their daughter. Lars seems to believe that his father was Bruno Schulz, a real-life Polish Jewish writer and school-teacher, who was murdered by the Germans during the Holocaust, just before Lars, an orphan from an orphan asylum, thinks he was born. It is known that Schulz's manuscript of an unpublished novel titled *The Messiah* was lost in the storm of Germanic ethnic cleansing. Andemening does not know who his mother was. He was adopted. Now he is learning Polish, supposedly his native language.

Lars is a literary scholar as well as an insomniac. Unlike his fellow reviewers, he likes to critique difficult texts from Central and Eastern Europe. His analyses are often Kafkaesque, and, therefore, his reviews are not popular. His taste in literature and his reclusiveness make him an "other," and thus half-way to being a Jew. Lars is a customer of Heidi Eklund, an acerbic owner of a small bookstore, whose mysterious husband, Dr. Eklund, is continually away at "conferences." Heidi slowly feeds Lars information about Schulz and shows him letters that the author had written. This keeps the reviewer coming back to the shop. Suddenly, Lars is informed by Heidi that he has a sister, Adela, and she is in Stockholm with the manuscript of *The Messiah*. Elated, Lars wants to believe that *The Messiah*, his father's book, which he has dreamed of finding, has come to Stockholm and to him.

Adela arrives at Lars's apartment carrying a bag, and she explains how she found out that she was Schulz's daughter. She shows him a little of the manuscript, and it seems to be in Schulz's handwriting, samples of which Heidi has sold to him. Lars asks Adela how she happened to have the same name of characters in Schulz's surviving books, and Adela informs him that Schulz gave her the name and used the name in his writing. Lars wants to hold the entire manuscript and read it, but Adela refuses. There is a scuffle. Adela is knocked down, but manages to escape with the manuscript.

Dr. Eklund finally appears in Heidi's shop, and Lars is surprised that Eklund has a Polish accent. Lars comes to learn that Eklund's real work is smuggling people out of Poland by forging passports. Adela is there too, and her voice sounds like Eklund's. He examines *The Messiah* manuscript as if he were a handwriting expert, and he assures Lars that it was written by Schulz. The Eklunds want Lars to translate the novel and publicize it through his review column. Lars is finally allowed to study the manuscript. The manuscript is fragmented, and the pages are out of order. Lars is distraught. He senses a forgery. He will not try to translate *The Messiah*. He realizes that the author of the manuscript is Eklund and Adela is his daughter, so Lars burns the manuscript. *The Messiah* has not come to Stockholm. The Eklunds are con artists.

Time passes and Adela, whose real married name is Elsa Vaz, visits Lars at the newspaper office accompanied by her infant son. She accuses Lars of picking a make believe father out of a book, and he accuses her of swiping the name Adela out of a book. Both have led fictional lives. She leaves with her child, and Lars grieves for his now dull, orphan life.

CHARACTER DEVELOPMENT

None of the five major characters in *The Messiah of Stockholm* are what they claim to be. The 42-year-old Lars Andemening so longs for an identity that he creates a fantasy father out of his reading about the death of Bruno Schulz, the Polish Jewish author killed by the Nazis in 1942. Lars's identity crisis ruins his life. It makes him a recluse. It destroys his two marriages. It causes his coworkers at the newspaper to think him an eccentric. Worst of all, it makes him vulnerable to the conniving Eklund family, who plan to use his desperate need to know more about his "father," Bruno Schulz, and his work, to con him into publicizing a forged partial manuscript—*The Messiah*—and make them wealthy. Lars is painfully torn between denying the probability that he is not Schulz's son and his need to know the truth. When Lars realizes he was nearly swindled, his life loses meaning and savor. As the son of a martyred Jew, he may have in a way believed himself to be the Messiah of Stockholm or at least the Messiah of Jewish memory.

Heidi Eklund, 65, white haired and overbearing, turns out to be German, not Swedish, and her bookstore, which never seems to have any customers but Lars, is a front for the family flimflams.

The elusive Dr. Eklund is awaited for much of the novel. Heidi continues to say that he is away at a conference. Lars and the reader never learn what kind of doctor he is, if indeed he is one. Toward the end of the narrative, when it is revealed that Eklund speaks Swedish with a Polish accent, and that his real work is forging passports and smuggling refugees out of Poland, it becomes obvious that he and Heidi are small-time criminals who have dragged Adela into their schemes. This unholy family is probably a refugee group that has landed in Sweden, just more debris from World War II.

Adela, whose real name turns out to be Elsa Vaz, is a pathetic character, a single mother, who has been drawn into the Eklunds' scheme. When she comes to Lars to confess, he is brutal to her, and she alone of the characters in the story provokes a little sympathy at the novel's conclusion. All of the characters live lives of self-deception or assume false identities.

THEMES

The Messiah of Stockholm is about how the Holocaust destroyed a culture as well as a significant portion of humanity. Lars Andemening, as a gentile Swede and a tabula rasa, and because he is an adopted orphan who never knew his biological parents, is able to take on the guilt of Western Christianity for complicity, through action or inaction, for the murder of six million innocent Jewish people in Europe in the mid-twentieth century. He does so by turning himself into the child of a victim trying to keep alive the memory of his murdered father. Ozick ironically indicates that because of the secularization of most contemporary Jews, their ancient culture is being lost, and the gentile world may have to sustain the memory of it. But a tradition so sustained can only be an artifice.

Additionally, *The Messiah of Stockholm* centers on the father figure, without which a human being is adrift, an arrested soul, someone seemingly incomplete and off the track of life. Without a family, one is always homeless and at a loss for a history. Orphaned and twice-divorced, Lars has no family. He has lost contact with his daughter, Karen, because the mother has taken the child to America. His child is growing up fatherless, while Lars's father and faith have been turned into pieces of paper.

Identity is a major theme in *The Messiah of Stockholm*. Questions are raised: How is an identity constructed? Is one's identity merely the accumulation of the myths and stories in one's memory? What is so special about a Jewish identity? Is it so different because of the unending suffering of the Jewish people? Does Jewish identity require a belief in the Messiah?

Ozick has deep respect for the Messianic tradition. She uses whiteness to symbolize it. The supposed manuscript of *The Messiah* is on white paper. Lars imagines Schulz, the author of *The Messiah*, as a prophet having an eye that emits violent white light flowing from God. Adela carries the manuscript in a white plastic bag, and when she leaves Lars for the last time, he throws her abandoned white beret after her, as if to say that all that is white—and thus pure—belong with the lost hope of the Messiah.

The Messiah of Stockholm presents the struggle between imagination and reason. Lars's reality is as thin as a piece of paper because in his existential life imagination has dominated reason. Ozick opines that many human beings are preoccupied, as is Lars, with living fraudulently, opting out of reality, afraid of truth. When the bubble of their fabricated self-image is burst, they are deeply wounded or set adrift like Lars Andemening.

NARRATIVE STYLE

The Messiah of Stockholm is a postmodern novel full of irony, borrowings of literary style from earlier writers (especially Franz Kafka), and shifting and twisting explanatory possibilities in the narrative. Ozick's playful metatextual teases include having Lars refer to an American review of Schulz's *The Street of Crocodiles*. Ozick wrote just such a review in 1977. Ozick's writing is sardonic, fierce, and totally unsentimental. Although Ozick employs the omniscient first-person narrative, the reader is quickly drawn into Lars's psychological life. Ozick skillfully employs suspense to sustain the narrative. The reader is never sure if a manuscript of *The Messiah* exists until the very end. As Lars is teased with glimpses of what is purported to be the lost manuscript written by his dead "father," he is lured further and further into the Eklunds' scam, and closer and closer to a life stripped of history, purpose, and meaning. *The Messiah of Stockholm* emphasizes the inner life of the protagonist, Lars Andemening, who once convinced himself that he was Jewish, and who may symbolize many contemporary nonobservant Jews who only play the part of being Jewish.

The Messiah of Stockholm is also a mystery story. What is Adela's real identity? Who and what are the Eklunds? Does Adela possess an authentic manuscript of *The Messiah*? As Heidi insists that *The Messiah* manuscript exists only if people believe it does, the manuscript symbolizes the Redeemer who will come one day to save Israel. Perhaps that Messiah exists only as long as people believe in the coming. Thus Lars's burning of the spurious manuscript is a symbolically religious act against a false redeemer.

HISTORICAL CONTEXT

On a trip to Stockholm in 1984 Ozick heard a thrilling rumor that Bruno Schulz's lost manuscript, *The Messiah*, had surfaced in that city. Ozick had been interested in Schulz's life and work since 1977 when Philip Roth informed her of the murdered author's writings. Schulz was shot dead on a street in the Polish city of Drohobycz, his native town, by a German S.S. officer. He had worked as a high school teacher and wrote on the side. In 1934, at the age of 40, he gained recognition as a writer of fiction with the publication of a collection of short stories, just as Ozick had achieved literary fame with *The Pagan Rabbi and Other Stories* in 1971.

Rumors emerging from Polish Jewish survivors of the Holocaust hinted that Schulz had been working on a novel titled *The Messiah* when he was murdered, and that a friend had hidden the possibly incomplete manuscript, but that it subsequently had been lost. This lost work surely seemed to Ozick to be symbolic of all the Jewish artistry obliterated by the Germans in the period in which they conquered and held most of Europe.

Schulz had translated Franz Kafka's great novel *The Trial* from German into Polish. Kafka is one of Ozick's most admired authors. In fact she has been fascinated and influenced by many Slavic Jewish authors of the twentieth century, including the Czech Kafka, the Russian Isaac Babel, and the Polish Isaac Bashevis Singer.

SUGGESTED READINGS

Primary Source

Ozick, Cynthia. *The Messiah of Stockholm*. New York: Knopf, 1987.

Secondary Sources

Cohen, Sarah Blacher. *Cynthia Ozick's Comic Art: From Levity to Liturgy*. Bloomington: Indiana University Press, 1994.

Friedman, Lawrence S. *Understanding Cynthia Ozick*. Columbia: University of South Carolina Press, 1991.

Kauver, Elaine M. *Cynthia Ozick's Fiction: Tradition and Invention*. Bloomington: University of Indiana Press, 1993.

Lowin, Joseph. *Cynthia Ozick*. Boston: Twayne, 1988.

Selected Bibliography

Antil, Mary. *The Promised Land*. New York: Houghton Mifflin, 1925.

Fischel, Jack, and Sanford Pinsker. *Jewish-American History and Culture: An Encyclopedia*. New York: Garland, 1992.

Freeman, Jonathan. *The Temple of Culture: Assimilation and Anti-Semitism in Literary America*. New York: Oxford University Press, 1999.

Fried, Lewis S., ed. *Handbook of American Jewish Literature*. Westport, Conn.: Greenwood, 1998.

Hapgood, Hutchins. *The Spirit of the Ghetto*. Cambridge, Mass.: Belknap Press of Harvard University, 1967. First published 1902 by Funk and Wagnalls.

Hertzberg, Arthur. *The Jew in America: Four Centuries of an Uneasy Encounter*. New York: Simon and Schuster, 1989.

Howe, Irving. *World of Our Fathers*. New York: Harcourt, Brace, Jovanovich, 1976.

Kramer, Michael P., and Hana Wirth-Nesher, eds. *The Cambridge Companion to Jewish American Literature*. Cambridge: Cambridge University Press, 2003.

Langer, Lawrence. *The Holocaust and the Literary Imagination*. New Haven, Conn.: Yale University Press, 1975.

Ludwig, Jack. *Recent American Novelists*. Madison: University of Wisconsin Press, 1966.

Moore, Deborah Dash. *At Home in America: Second Generation New York Jews*. New York: Columbia University Press, 1981.

Ozick, Cynthia. *Metaphor and Memory*. New York: Vintage, 1989.

Pinsker, Sanford. *Jewish-American Fiction, 1917–1987*. New York: Twayne, 1992.

Samuel, Maurice. *The World of Sholem Aleichem*. New York: Knopf, 1943.

Shapiro, Ann R., ed. *Jewish American Women Writers: A Bibliographic and Critical Sourcebook*. Westport, Conn.: Greenwood, 1994.

Shatzky, Joel, and Michael Taub, eds. *Contemporary Jewish-American Writers: A Bio-Critical Sourcebook*. Westport, Conn.: Greenwood, 1997.

Wade, Stephen. *Jewish American Literature Since 1945*. Chicago: Fitzroy Dearborn, 1999.

Weinberg, Sydney Stahl. *The World of Our Mothers: The Lives of Jewish Immigrant Women*. New York: Shocken, 1988.

Wisse, Ruth R. *The Modern Jewish Canon: A Journey Through Language and Culture*. New York: The Free Press, 2000.

Index

About the Author

SANFORD STERNLICHT is Professor of English at Syracuse University. He has published several books of poetry, and his scholarly studies include *A Reader's Guide to Modern Irish Drama* (1998), *Chaim Potok: A Critical Companion* (Greenwood, 2000), *Student Companion to Elie Wiesel* (Greenwood, 2003), and *Masterpieces of Modern British and Irish Drama* (Greenwood, 2005).